Y0-BWG-681

AUGUST 1977 Volume 28/Number 5

AMERICAN HERITAGE

Sponsored by American Association for State and Local History • Society of American Historians

AMERICAN HERITAGE, The Magazine of History, is published every two months by American Heritage Publishing Co., Inc.; editorial and executive offices, 10 Rockefeller Plaza, N.Y., N.Y. 10020. Secretary, Anthony J. Sansiveri. Correspondence about subscriptions should go to American Heritage Subscription Office, 383 West Center St., Marion, Ohio 43302. Single copies: $6. Annual subscriptions: $24 in U.S. and Canada; $26 elsewhere. A 10-year Index of Vols. VI-XV is available at $7.50; 5-year Index of Vols. XVI-XX at $7.50; 5-year Index of Vols. XXI-XXV at $7.50.

AMERICAN HERITAGE considers but assumes no responsibility for unsolicited materials; these require return postage. Title registered U.S. Patent Office. Second-class postage paid at New York, N.Y., and at additional mailing offices.

Postmaster: Please send Form 3579 to AMERICAN HERITAGE, 381 West Center Street, Marion, Ohio 43302.

AMERICAN HERITAGE has been selected by the Library of Congress for reproduction on recordings called Talking Books, distributed free by regional libraries in the U.S. to those unable to use conventional print because of a visual or physical handicap. For information write the Library of Congress, Division for the Blind and Physically Handicapped, 1291 Taylor St., N.W., Washington, D.C. 20542.

CONTENTS

4 God's "Almost Chosen People"
Martin E. Marty

8 Who Started the Cold War?
1. A Good Way to Pick a Fight
Charles L. Mee, Jr.
2. "We Can't Do Business With Stalin"
W. Averell Harriman and Elie Abel
3. Mr. Mee Replies

24 Route 66: Ghost Road of the Okies
Thomas W. Pew, Jr.

36 The U.S. vs. International Terrorists: A Chapter From Our Past
Gaddis Smith

44 American Characters: Nikola Tesla
Nat Brandt

46 The Adventures of a Haunted Whaling Man
A Diary of 1855–58

66 George Washington Carver and the Peanut: New Light on a Much-Loved Myth
Barry Mackintosh

74 Images of War
Jimmy Hare's Photojournalism

82 Hollywood's Garden of Allah
George Oppenheimer

88 An Immodest Proposal: Nikita to Adlai
John Bartlow Martin

90 The Hinckley Fire
Richard F. Snow

97 The Way I See It
Bruce Catton

98 Jack London—The Man Who Invented Himself
Andrew Sinclair

108 Readers' Album: High Camp

109 Crossword Puzzle
The Old West

110 Postscripts

COVER

Front: Presidential nominee Jimmy Carter and family in prayer at the Democratic Convention, July 15, 1976. (The woman at the left in the full photo is convention chairman Lindy Boggs.) A provocative article about the remarkable persistence of America's religious faith begins on page 4.

DAVID BURNETT/CONTACT

Back: A quintessentially American summer scene is depicted in this detail from *County Fair,* painted by Chicago artist Frederick M. Grant about 1915.

UNION LEAGUE CLUB OF CHICAGO

FRONTISPIECE

Edward Moran's splendid painting shows the U.S. frigate *Philadelphia* being destroyed by the American naval hero Stephen Decatur in the harbor of Tripoli in 1804. For an explanation, see page 36.

UNITED STATES NAVAL ACADEMY MUSEUM

GOD'S "ALMOST CHOSEN PEOPLE"

by Martin E. Marty

"We are a religious people. . . ." The United States Supreme Court likes to quote this dictum by Justice William O. Douglas, who coined the phrase to accompany a decision in 1952. The Court has not been trying to provide America's pious Little Jack Horners with new reasons to say, "What a good boy am I!" The justices are not supposed to favor particular religions or to discriminate against irreligion. They merely have been explaining why their legal decisions take into account the sentiments of so many citizens on the delicate subject of religion.

Two centuries ago seers might have had good reason to expect the court one day to say, "We are a secular people. . . ." The charter for the new nation was secular, or nonreligious. Its Constitution differed from the written covenants of other nations because it committed no one to a religious faith. Nine of the thirteen original colonies had tried to perpetuate age-old European practices in which citizens were taxed for the support of privileged churches, but these establishments were soon to crumble. The First Amendment to the Constitution asked for congressional hands off where religion was concerned. Only a small percentage of the citizens then belonged to or attended churches, and the philosophy of the Enlightenment often beckoned the educated away from conventional forms of religion.

Two hundred years later, few protested when the Court, against that background, judged that "we are a religious people," and not many would fail to recognize themselves in this portrait of the nation. But it is appropriate to ask, "Religious compared to whom?" Since the American majority traced its ancestry to Europe, backward glances across the Atlantic have always been revealing. Ever since Alexis de Tocqueville in the 1830's, European visitors have come expecting to find a pagan America and have left dazzled by the varieties of our religiosity. By contrast, recent American travelers revisiting Christendom's monuments in Europe have reported back that the cathedrals were empty and the people ignoring their historic faith. Europe's religion sometimes seems little more than a memory, an item for the museums.

In recent years, as the art or science of poll-taking began to be refined, interviewers provided harder data to support the impressions of the trans-Atlantic commuters. The Gallup Opinion Index, for example, made news in the bicentennial year of the American republic with an account of ten thousand international interviews. People were asked, "How important to you are your religious beliefs?" and whether they believed in "God or a universal spirit" and in "life after death."

India, still steeped in its traditional Hindu and Islamic traditions, turned out to have the most religious respondents. But among the industrialized nations, concerning which there was most curiosity, United States citizens gave impressive support to the Supreme Court's observation. Trailing far behind in these three indices of religiosity were neighboring Canada and then a variety of European nations, Australia, and industrial Japan.

In the United States 94 per cent believed in God, while only 72 per cent of the French and West German people expressed the same faith. Fifty-six per cent of the Americans polled found religious beliefs to be "very important," while only 36 per cent in Catholic Italy, 23 per cent in the United Kingdom, and 12 per cent in Japan made the same claim. On immortality, 69 per cent of the Americans were positive, while only 43 per cent in the United Kingdom and 18 per cent of the Japanese answered yes, they believed.

Slice the sample any way you wish. Take college-educated citizens. In the United States 49 per cent found religion to be "very important," while in western Europe only 24 per cent did; 91 per cent of America's college-educated believed in God, but only 76 per cent of the Europeans did; the 66 per cent of America's college-bred who believed in immortality were balanced by only 46 per cent of the Europeans who had gone to college and still looked forward to an alumni association that lasted beyond the mortal years.

Polls are often flawed. Samples can be skewed. Statistics may mislead. Those who answer interviewers can deceive themselves. But with all reservations made, fingers crossed, and brows skeptically furrowed, interpreters agree that here is more evidence of the fact that Americans cherish the image of piety and want to give evidence that they embody it. So decisive are all the returns that thoughtful observers move on almost at once from questions regarding *whether* Americans are religious, to *why* they are.

Ask the promoters of organized religion why faith has prospered in America, and they will likely agree with Jonathan Edwards. In the Great Awakening year of 1738 the minister wrote of his Northampton: "The beginning of the late work of God in this place was so circumstanced that I could not but look upon it as a remarkable testimony of God's approbation" of New England's pattern of belief. No wonder Edwards could write "faithful narratives" of "the Surprizing Work of God in the Conversions of Many... Souls...." Since 68 per cent of the citizens tell Dr. Gallup that God "observes their actions and rewards and punishes them for them," it is plausible that many would still give God credit for their visibly religious character. But such an explanation does not rule out others and does little to explain why the Deity has granted Americans "most favored nation" status.

More mundane explanations of America's pattern should begin with the formula chosen by the new nation about two centuries ago. The act of "separating church from state" removed most occasions for public resentment of formal religion. Anti-clericalism has consequently seldom been an agent of political partisanship in America as it has been, say, in Spain or Mexico. The Founding Fathers, in separating the civil from the religious sphere, made religion an escapable choice, something that could also be more attractive than when it was forced upon their ancestors. Thrown on their own resources, the churches had to win Americans' hearts.

Charters and formulas for freedom do not make people religious. They only allow for them to be nonreligious or to be pious in an infinitely rich number of ways. Americans needed and possessed other assets. First among these was the landscape itself, the vast map of open spaces for refuge, colonizing, pioneering, building cities and utopias, fashioning new communities, and providing isolation for those who wanted to stay away from people of other religious outlooks. Certainly, they thought, God spoke through the environment with its "templed hills." But human resources were even more impressive, as endless varieties of believers from Europe, Africa, and Asia came and had to make sense of that environment.

As the various peoples arrived, they brought along some traditions to forget and then chose to remember many of them. They eventually left behind most of their ancient and tribal customs, Old World languages and customs and recipes. But through the centuries they kept on having to ask who they were in this new and bewildering place. To whom and to what did they belong in a mobile society? What might they hope for in a culture that inspired so many competing dreams?

Given such resources and needs, *why* are we a "religious people"? Conservatives will be offended by one plausible answer, and progressives by a different version of the same. Conservatives first. They have warred against evolutionary theories since before Darwin, but in religious life they live out an example of evolutionary development. By evolution here I mean

MICHAEL PHILIP MANHEIM—PHOTO RESEARCHERS

MARC RIBOUD—MAGNUM

SUSAN MCCARTNEY—PHOTO RESEARCHERS

TOM HOLLYMAN—PHOTO RESEARCHERS

DAN BUDNIK—WOODFIN CAMP & ASSOCIATES

TOBY RANKIN—THE IMAGE BANK

ELLIOTT ERWITT—MAGNUM

BRUCE FRISCH—PHOTO RESEARCHERS

JOHN V. NEAL—PHOTO RESEARCHERS

something far more subtle than the crude motifs of "natural selection" and the "survival of the fittest," though these have also been visible in American piety. Evolution rather refers to the ability of religious groups to adapt to their complex environments with ever more complex forms. Eventually they came up with a "church of your choice" for almost everyone, with a cafeteria line of spiritual options for most tastes, and with custom-made faiths for every kind of customer and consumer.

American religious history is a stunning story of adaptation and diversification of choices. In the early nineteenth century, the earnestly pious set out to reform the nation. They developed answers to questions yet dimly asked, cures for diseases only vaguely then felt, solutions to problems only rarely yet perceived. People invented societies for all purposes, to the ultimate point of forming local branches of the London Society for Providing Trusses for the Ruptured Poor. Ever since, religious decline would have spelled trouble for reform of society or voluntary action to improve it. From abolition through the clerical activism of recent years, the pious have agitated on both sides of most worthwhile disputes. Even today people channel far more than half their charitable dollars through religious agencies, and give more than half their hours of voluntary service to churches.

In quiet ways religion is locked into too many parts of too many peoples' lives to slip easily away. Churches and synagogues may be more than burial societies, but they are at least that. They also provide outlets for the expression of egos, places to be seen and accepted, occasions for spiritual enjoyment, and where they do this well there is little danger of their decline. European clerics, by contrast, talk ruefully about apathetic life in tail-ending establishments. There, some say, people come to church only on the four wheels of baby carriages for christening, limousines for marriage, and hearses for burials—to be "hatched, matched, and dispatched."

Established European religion did far less adapting and diversifying. After World War II, for example, we heard much of the lay renewal in Christian Europe. In 1960 I thought it timely to seek out the traces. Typically, a Dutch cleric showed me a new room with a table and eight chairs that was attached to his old church. It was, he said, "the locale of our lay emphasis." A thriving American church would have had a gymnasium, credit union, nursery, art galleries, business office, senior citizens' center, sanctuary, and bookstore.

Religious liberals, not always friends of the competitive free market, will not enjoy seeing it credited with helping provide for their religious prosperity. Americans, in such a reading, are religious because competitive religious groups have successfully exploited every changing taste and need. The capitalist model inspired a century of competition and lived on in an ecumenical age when milder-mannered leaders became uneasy over the churches' efforts to do each other in.

When the American West was opened, Baptists, Methodists, and Disciples of Christ lunged at each other as they raced to overwhelm the old colonial denominations—the Congregationalists, Episcopalians, and Presbyterians—and to keep Catholics at bay or away. When boatloads of later Europeans arrived, they were often only nominal Catholics or Protestants, but priests and missionaries met their boats, cajoled them into showing loyalty, and inspired them to activity. When conventional options did not offer the right products, new religions arose: Mormon, Adventist, Christian Scientist, Jehovah's Witnessing, Theosophist. Blacks turned the church into the chief zone of their common life. Dispersed Jews often converged on synagogues. It was not easy to escape the nets thrown out by religions of all sorts. Today new groups derived from Asian, African, or occult sources have borrowed the familiar aggressive tactics of Western faiths.

Competition and divisiveness have been played down at least since 1908, when the Protestants' Federal Council of Churches was formed, and certainly since the Catholics' Second Vatican Council in the 1960's. Jews have sought "brotherhood" through the years. The spiritual climate is generally friendlier. Still, in 1972 Dean M. Kelley provided shock treatment for brotherhood's shock troops when he showed in *Why Conservative Churches Are Growing* that it was the blatantly competitive and unfriendly churches that prospered in the new market.

Consumer-oriented religion has finally become so custom-made that in America's free climate there seem to be not simply as many religions as there are churches—over 220 in the *Yearbook of American Churches*—but as there are citizens. German sociologist Thomas Luckmann speaks of "the invisible religion," the faith that survives in the high-rise apartment or over the long weekend, far from rabbi, priest, and minister. This is the spirituality of the do-it-yourself American religionists who blend a completely private mix of everything from astrology to Zen, of mail-ordered, televised, and Great Booked options that satisfy their own search for meaning even if the result cannot easily be transmitted to others or to new generations.

Not everyone has taken such private religion lying down. Racial, ethnic, and denominational groups have been talking again the common language of tribe and peoplehood. Public philosophers from Benjamin Franklin in 1749 with his "publick Religion" to Robert Bellah and his "civil religion" in 1967 have tried to minister to the American hunger for wholeness. "We are a religious people," and many of us do come together around occasions provided by presidential inaugural addresses, public holidays, and elementary-school ceremonies. Major writers took the old biblical language about God's elect people and Americanized it. Thus Herman Melville boasted: "We Americans are the peculiar, chosen people—the Israel of our time; we bear the ark of the liberties of the world." Even Abraham Lincoln thought his were God's "almost chosen people." Such language by fusing spirituality with national purpose contributed to our sense of mission and manifest destiny, thus assuring religion a secure place whenever Americans have wanted to take on something for which they needed courage.

When the arrival of religious freedom brought the possibility of freedom *from* religion two centuries ago, few citizens lost faith and many gained it. With the onset of modernity, whatever it was supposed to mean, prophets predicted the death of God and the demise of religion. Not all believers try to account for God's ways, but religion itself did not die. It was simply relocated, sometimes disguised, busy seeking to fill society's many nooks and crannies that offer growth to both old and new religious organizations and private emphases. If the polls are correct, few are trying to evade religion's claims or appeals. So long as citizens seek freedom and justice, hunger to be whole, want to be saved, and wish to know who they are and to whom they belong, many are likely to find new ways to give support to the Court's claim that "we are a religious people." The American majority, for all their secular styles and worldly concerns, are likely to see in such expressions what Jonathan Edwards perceived in the 1730's, "the Surprizing Work of God." And they will gladly say so to Dr. Gallup or anyone else who asks.

Martin E. Marty teaches at the University of Chicago, is an editor of The Christian Century, *and has recently published* A Nation of Behavers *(University of Chicago Press).*

F.B. GRUNZWEIG—PHOTO RESEARCHERS

TIM EAGAN—WOODFIN CAMP & ASSOCIATES

M. NAYTHONS—LIAISON

JAN LUKAS—RAPHO/PHOTO RESEARCHERS

JOHN SULLIVAN—PHOTO RESEARCHERS

LARRY FRIED—THE IMAGE BANK

ANDREW SACKS—GAMMA/LIAISON

ELLIOTT ERWITT—MAGNUM

STAN PANTOVIC—PHOTO RESEARCHERS

ROBERT FARBER—THE IMAGE BANK

ROGER MALLOCH—MAGNUM

WINSTON VARGAS—PHOTO RESEARCHERS

KATRINA THOMAS—PHOTO RESEARCHERS

MARGARET DURRANCE—PHOTO RESEARCHERS

DAN GURAVICH—PHOTO RESEARCHERS

WHO STARTED THE COLD WAR?

The Cold War—we have spent a generation hearing about it, thinking about it, worrying about it. We all know it somehow grew out of World War II, that it involved conflict between the United States and the Soviet Union, and that it led to a series of frightening confrontations: the Berlin airlift; the escalating stages of the nuclear arms race; the Cuban missile crisis; the wars in Korea and Vietnam. But what really *caused* the Cold War? It is not a simple question, and knowledgeable and honest men can differ considerably in answering it.

On the following pages, Charles L. Mee, Jr., formerly editor of HORIZON magazine and the author of *Meeting at Potsdam* (1975) and, currently, *A Visit to Haldeman and Other States of Mind*, presents an unorthodox view of how the Cold War began. He is replied to by W. Averell Harriman, former U.S. ambassador to the Soviet Union and a distinguished participant in some of the relevant events, writing in collaboration with Elie Abel, dean of the Columbia University School of Journalism; finally Mr. Mee is given space for a brief rebuttal. It all adds up, we think, to a most thoughtful and provocative consideration of an awesome fact of the modern world that has overshadowed our lives and our children's lives, and will continue to do so.

LOUIS GOLDMAN, RAPHO/PHOTO RESEARCHERS

1. A Good Way to Pick a Fight

by Charles L. Mee, Jr.

On April 12, 1945, Franklin Roosevelt died, and soon afterward Vyascheslav M. Molotov, the Russian foreign minister, stopped by in Washington to pay his respects to Harry Truman, the new President. Truman received Molotov in the Oval Office and, as Truman recalled it, chewed him out "bluntly" for the way the Russians were behaving in Poland. Molotov was stunned. He had never, he told Truman, "been talked to like that in my life."

"Carry out your agreements," Truman responded, "and you won't get talked to like that."

That's a good way to talk, if you want to start an argument...

In Europe, Germany surrendered to the Allies on May 8. On May 12, Prime Minister Winston Churchill sent Truman an ominous cable about the Russians: "An iron curtain is drawn down upon their front," Churchill said, and, moreover, "it would be open to the Russians in a very short time to advance if they chose to the waters of the North Sea and the Atlantic." On May 17, Churchill ordered his officers not to destroy any German planes. In fact, Churchill kept 700,000 captured German troops in military readiness, prepared to be turned against the Russians.

That, too, is a good way to behave, if you are looking for trouble...

Joseph Stalin said little: he did not advance his troops to the Atlantic, but he planted them firmly throughout eastern Europe and, in violation of previous agreements with the British and Americans, systematically crushed all vestiges of democratic government in Poland, Hungary, Czechoslovakia, Bulgaria, Rumania, Yugoslavia, and Finland. In truth, not quite: the Finns had managed to salvage a few bits and scraps of democratic usage for themselves. At dinner one night in the Kremlin, Andrei Zhdanov, one of Stalin's propagandists, complained that the Russians should have occupied Finland. "Akh, Finland," said Molotov, "that is a peanut."

And that, too, is a nice way to behave, if you are trying to stir up a fight...

Most people, most of the time, want peace in the world, and they imagine that most politicians, being human, share the same wishes. At the end of a war, presumably, the desire for peace is most intense and most widely shared. Lamentably, that is not always the case. At the end of World War II the Russians, as Churchill remarked, feared "our friendship more than our enmity."

The Russians had both immediate cause and long-standing historical reasons for anxiety.

"From the beginning of the ninth century," as Louis Halle, a former State Department historian, has written, "and even today, the prime driving force in Russia has been fear.... The Russians as we know them today have experienced ten centuries of constant, mortal fear. This has not been a disarming experience. It has not been an experience calculated to produce a simple, open, innocent, and guileless society." Scattered over a vast land with no natural frontiers for protection, as Halle remarks, the Russians have been overrun "generation after generation, by fresh waves of invaders.... Lying defenseless on the plain, they were slaughtered and subjugated and humiliated by the invaders time and again."

Thus the Russians sought to secure their borders along eastern Europe. The czars attempted this, time and again: to secure a buffer zone, on their European frontier, a zone that would run down along a line that would later be called the Iron Curtain.

Yet, at the end of World War II, Stalin's fears were not just fears of outsiders. World War II had shown that his dictatorship was not only brutal but also brutally inept; he was neither a great military leader nor a good administrator; and the Russian soldiers returning from the Western Front had seen much evidence of Western prosperity. Stalin needed the Cold War, not to venture out into the world again after an exhausting war, but to discipline his restless people at home. He had need of that ancient stratagem of monarchs—the threat of an implacable external enemy to be used to unite his own people in Russia.

Churchill, on the other hand, emerged from World War II with a ruined empire irretrievably in debt, an empire losing its colonies and headed inevitably toward bankruptcy. Churchill's scheme for saving Great Britain was suitably inspired and grand: he would, in effect, reinvent the British Empire; he would establish an economic union of Europe (much like what the Common Market actually became); this union would certainly not be led by vanquished Germany or Italy, not by so small a power as the Netherlands, not by devastated France, but by Great Britain. To accomplish this aim, unfortunately, Churchill had almost nothing in the way of genuine economic or military power left; he had only his own force of persuasion and rhetoric. He would try to parlay those gifts into American backing for England's move into Europe. The way to bring about American backing was for Churchill to arrange to have America and Russia quarrel; while America and Russia quarreled, England would—as American diplomats delicately put it—"lead" Europe.

Truman, for his part, led a nation that was strong and getting stronger. Henry Luce, the publisher of the influential *Time* and *Life* magazines, declared that this was to be the beginning of "the American Century"—and such a moment is rarely one in which a national leader wants to maintain a status quo. The United States was securing the Western Hemisphere, moving forcefully into England's collapsing "sterling bloc," acquiring military and economic positions over an area of the planet so extensive that the sun could never set on it.

The promise was extraordinary, the threat equally so. The United States did not practice Keynesian economics during the 1930's. It was not Roosevelt's New Deal that ran up the enormous federal deficit or built the huge, wheezing federal bureaucracy of today. War ran up the deficit; war licked the depression; war made the big federal government. In 1939, after a decade of depression, after the Civilian Conservation Corps, the Public Works Administration, the Civil Works Administration, the Agricultural Adjustment Act, the Social Security Act, and all the rest of the New Deal efforts on behalf of social justice, the federal budget was $9 billion. In 1945 it was $100 billion.

American prosperity was built upon deficit spending for war. President Truman knew it, and maintained deficit spending with the Cold War. Eventually, with the Truman Doctrine and the Marshall Plan, the encouragement of American multinational companies, and a set of defense treaties that came finally to encompass the world, he institutionalized it. The American people might find this easier to damn if they had not enjoyed the uncommon prosperity it brought them.

In October, 1944, Churchill visited Stalin in Moscow. The need then, clearly, was for cooperation among the Allies in order to win the war—and it appeared at the time that the cooperativeness nurtured during the war could be continued afterward. Each had only to recognize the other's vital interests. Churchill commenced to outline those interests to be recognized for the sake of the postwar cooperation.

"I said," Churchill recalled, "'Let us settle about our affairs in the Balkans. Your armies are in Rumania and Bulgaria. We have interests, missions, and agents there. Don't let us get at cross-purposes in small ways. So far as Britain and Russia are concerned, how would it do for you to have ninety per cent predominance in Rumania, for us to have ninety per cent of the say in Greece, and go fifty-fifty about Yugoslavia?'"

Churchill wrote this out on a piece of paper, noting, too, a split of Bulgaria that gave Russia 75 per cent interest, and a fifty-fifty split of Hungary. He pushed the piece of paper across the table to Stalin, who placed a check mark on it and handed it back. There was a silence. "At length I said, 'Might it not be thought rather cynical if it seemed we had disposed of these issues, so fateful to millions of people, in such an offhand manner? Let us burn the paper.' 'No, you keep it,' said Stalin."

Such casual and roughshod "agreements" could hardly be the last word on the matter; yet, they signified a mutual recognition of one another's essential interests and a willingness to accommodate one another's needs—while, to be sure, the smaller powers were sold out by all sides. At this same time, in October, 1944, and later on in January, 1945, Roosevelt entered into armistice agreements with Britain and Russia that gave Stalin almost complete control of the internal affairs of the ex-Nazi satellites in eastern Europe. As a briefing paper that the State Department prepared in the spring of 1945 for President Truman said, "spheres of influence do in fact exist," and "eastern Europe is, in fact, a Soviet sphere of influence."

In short, the stage was set for postwar peace: spheres of influence had been recognized; a tradition of negotiation had been established. Yet, the European phase of World War II was no sooner ended than symptoms of the Cold War began to appear. The Big Three no longer needed one another to help in the fight against Hitler, and the atomic bomb would soon settle the war against Japan.

Toward the end of May, 1945, Harry Hopkins arrived in Moscow to talk with Stalin, to feel out the Russians now that the war in Europe had ended, and to prepare the agenda for discussion at the Potsdam Conference that would be held in Germany in mid-July. The United States had a problem, Hopkins informed Stalin, a problem so serious that it threatened "to affect adversely the relations between our two countries." The problem was, Hopkins said, Poland: "our inability to carry into effect the Yalta Agreement on Poland."

But, what was the problem? Stalin wanted to know. A government had been established there, under the auspices of the occupying Red Army, a government that was, naturally, "friendly" to the Soviet Union. There could be no problem—unless others did not wish to allow the Soviet Union to ensure a friendly government in Poland.

"Mr. Hopkins stated," according to the notes taken by his interpreter, Charles Bohlen, "that the United States would desire a Poland friendly to the Soviet Union and in fact desired to see friendly countries all along the Soviet borders.

"Marshal Stalin replied if that be so we can easily come to terms in regard to Poland."

But, said Hopkins, Stalin must remember the Declaration on Liberated Europe (signed at the Yalta Conference in February, 1945) and its guarantees for democratic governments; here was a serious difference between them; Poland had become the issue over which cooperation between Russia and America would flourish or fail.

Evidently Stalin could not understand this demand; apparently he could not believe that Americans were sincerely so idealistic. Did not America, after all, support a manifestly undemocratic dictatorship in Franco's Spain? "I am afraid," Averell Harriman, the U.S. ambassador to the Soviet Union, cabled home to Truman, "Stalin does not and never will fully understand our interest in a

Big Three at Potsdam, 1945
BILL BELKNAP. RAPHO/PHOTO RESEARCHERS

free Poland as a matter of principle. He is a realist in all of his actions, and it is hard for him to appreciate our faith in abstract principles. It is difficult for him to understand why we should want to interfere with Soviet policy in a country like Poland, which he considers so important to Russia's security, unless we have some ulterior motive."

And indeed, Russia's sphere of influence was recognized, it seemed, only so that it might serve as a bone of contention. Poland, Czechoslovakia, Bulgaria, Rumania, Hungary, all became bones of contention. It is not clear that any one of the Big Three deeply cared what happened to these eastern European countries so long as the countries served as useful pawns. Hopkins insisted that Stalin must recognize freedom of speech, assembly, movement, and religious worship in Poland and that all political parties (except fascists) must be "permitted the free use, without distinction, of the press, radio, meetings and other facilities of political expression." Furthermore, all citizens must have "the right of public trial, defense by counsel of their own choosing, and the right of habeas corpus."

Of course, Stalin said, of course, "these principles of democracy are well known and would find no objection on the part of the Soviet Government." To be sure, he said, "in regard to the *specific* [italics added] freedoms mentioned by Mr. Hopkins, they could only be applied in full in peace time, and even then with certain limitations."

In the latter two weeks of July, 1945, the Big Three gathered at Potsdam, just outside of Berlin, for the last of the wartime conferences. They discussed the issues with which the war in Europe had left them, and with which the war in the Far East would leave them when it came to an end. They discussed spheres of influence, the disposition of Germany, the spoils of war, reparations, and, of course, eastern Europe.

At one of the plenary sessions of the Potsdam Conference, they outlined the spheres of influence precisely, clearly, and in detail during a discussion of the issue of "German shares, gold, and assets abroad." To whom did these items belong? What, for instance, did Stalin mean when he said "abroad"?

STALIN: ". . . the Soviet delegation . . . will regard the whole of Western Germany as falling within your sphere, and Eastern Germany, within ours."

Truman asked whether Stalin meant to establish "a line running from the Baltic to the Adriatic." Stalin replied that he did.

STALIN: "As to the German investments, I should put the question this way: as to the German investments in Eastern Europe, they remain with us, and the rest, with you. . . ."

TRUMAN: "Does this apply only to German investments in Europe or in other countries as well?"

STALIN: "Let me put it more specifically: the German investments in Rumania, Bulgaria, Hungary, and Finland go to us, and all the rest to you."

FOREIGN MINISTER ERNEST BEVIN: "The German investments in other countries go to us?"

STALIN: "In all other countries, in South America, in Canada, etc., all this is yours. . . ."

SECRETARY OF STATE JAMES BYRNES: "If an enterprise is not in Eastern Europe but in Western Europe or in other parts of the world, that enterprise remains ours?"

STALIN: "In the United States, in Norway, in Switzerland, in Sweden, in Argentina [general laughter], etc.—all that is yours."

A delegation of Poles arrived at Potsdam to argue their own case before the Big Three. The Poles, struggling desperately and vainly for their land, their borders, their freedoms, did not seem to understand that their fate was being settled for reasons that had nothing to do with them. They wandered about Potsdam, trying to impress their wishes on the Big Three. "I'm sick of the bloody Poles," Churchill said when they came to call on him. "I don't want to see them. Why can't Anthony [Eden] talk to them?" Alexander Cadogan, Permanent Undersecretary for Foreign Affairs, found the Poles at Eden's house late one night and "had to entertain them as best I could, and went on entertaining them—no signs of A. He didn't turn up till 11:30. . . . So then we got down to it, and talked shop till 1:30. Then filled the Poles (and ourselves) with sandwiches and whiskies and sodas and I went to bed at 2 A.M." Altogether, it had been an agreeable enough evening, although in general, Cadogan confided to his diary, he found the Poles to be "dreadful people. . . ."

Germany, too, provided a rich field for contention. The answer to the German question became a simple but ticklish matter of keeping Germany sufficiently weak so that it could not start another war and yet, at the same time, sufficiently strong to serve as a buffer against Russia, or, from Russia's point of view, against the Western powers. To achieve this delicate balance, the Big Three haggled at Potsdam over a complex set of agreements about zones of authority, permissible levels of postwar industry, allocation of resources of coal and foodstuffs, spoils of war, reparations, and other matters. The country as a whole was divided into administrative zones in which Allied commanders had absolute veto powers over some matters, and, in other respects, had to defer to a central governmental council for measures to be applied uniformly to Germany.

Out of all these careful negotiations came the astonishing fact that Germany was established as the very center and source of much of the anxiety and conflict of the Cold War. How this could

Below: Marshall Plan, 1947
U.P.I.

Right: Berlin Airlift, 1948
WAHER SANDERS FOR *Life* MAGAZINE, © TIME INC.

have happened is one of the wonders of the history of diplomacy. The discussions and bargaining at Potsdam among Churchill, Truman, and Stalin, and among the foreign ministers, and on lower levels, among economic committees and subcommittees, is maddeningly tangled; but, once all of the nettlesome complexities are cleared away, the postwar arrangement for Germany can be seen with sudden and arresting clarity. The Big Three agreed to have a Germany that would be politically united–but, at the very same time, economically divided. They agreed, then, to create a country that could never be either wholly united nor entirely divided, neither one Germany nor two Germanies, but rather a country that would be perpetually at war with itself, and, since its two halves would have two patrons, would keep its two patrons in continuous conflict. Whether this postwar arrangement for Germany was intentional or inadvertent, it was certainly a diplomatic tour de force. In 1949, with the formation of the West German and East German governments, the contradictions of the Potsdam policy became overt.

Eastern Europe, Germany, and the atomic bomb were the three most striking elements of the early Cold War. It was while he was at the Potsdam Conference that President Truman received news that the test of the bomb at Alamogordo had been successful. By that time the bomb was no longer militarily necessary to end the war against Japan; the Japanese were near the end and were attempting to negotiate peace by way of their ambassador to Moscow. After the bomb was dropped, Truman would maintain that it had avoided the invasion of the Japanese mainland and so saved a million American lives. But was that true?

General Henry (Hap) Arnold, chief of the Army Air Forces, said, before the atomic device was dropped on Japan, that conventional bombing would end the war without an invasion. Admiral Ernest J. King, chief of U.S. naval operations, advised that a naval blockade alone would end the war. General Eisenhower said it was "completely unnecessary" to drop the bomb, and that the weapon was "no longer mandatory as a measure to save American lives." Even General George Marshall, U.S. chief of staff and the strongest advocate at that late hour for the bomb's use, advised that the Japanese at least be forewarned to give them a chance to surrender. Diplomats advised Truman that he need only have Russia sign his proclamation calling for Japanese surrender; the Russians had not yet declared war against Japan, and so the Japanese still had hopes that the Russians would help them negotiate peace; if Russia signed the proclamation, the Japanese would see that their last chance was gone and would surrender. None of this advice was followed.

After the war, the United States Strategic Bombing Command issued a study confirming the advice Truman had been getting before he gave the order to drop the atomic bomb: "Japan would have surrendered even if the atomic bombs had not been dropped, even if Russia had not entered the war, and even if no invasion had been planned or contemplated." Then why was it dropped? Admiral William Leahy, Truman's top aide, was unable to offer the puzzled British chiefs of staff a better explanation than that it was "because of the vast sums that had been spent on the project," although he commented that in using the bomb, the Americans "had adopted an ethical standard common to the barbarians of the Dark Ages."

However that may be, its use must have been chilling to Stalin; doubly chilling if Stalin realized that the United States had used the bomb even when it was not militarily necessary. Indeed, according to Secretary of State James Byrnes, that was the real reason why the bomb was used after all–"to make Russia," as he said, "more manageable in Europe." Perhaps it is because that constituted a war crime–to kill people when it is not militarily necessary is a war crime according to international accord–that Truman insisted to his death, and in obstinate defiance of all other opinion, that it was militarily necessary.

The bomb may have been dropped, too, in order to end the war against Japan without Russian help. The Russians had promised to enter the war in the Far East exactly three months after the war in Europe ended–which it did on May 8. Truman's aim was not merely to end the war against Japan, but to end it before August 8.

When word reached Potsdam that the atomic bomb had been successfully tested, Truman was enormously pleased. When the news was passed along to Churchill, the prime minister was overcome with delight at the "vision–fair and bright indeed it seemed–of the end of the whole war in one or two violent shocks." Churchill understood at once that "we should not need the Russians," and he concluded that "we seemed suddenly to have become possessed of a merciful abridgment of the slaughter in the East and of a far happier prospect in Europe. I have no doubt that these thoughts were present in the minds of my American friends."

The problem was what to tell the Russians. Presumably, as allies of the Americans and British, they needed to be told of this new weapon in which Truman and Churchill placed such tremendous hopes. Yet, if the Russians were told, they might rush to enter the war against Japan and so share in the victory. "The President and I no longer felt that we needed [Stalin's] aid to conquer Japan," Churchill wrote. And so Stalin must be told about the existence of the bomb–and at the same time he must not be told. In short, Truman and Churchill decided, Stalin must be informed so casually as not to understand that he was being

Left: North Atlantic Treaty Organization, 1949

Below: Korea, 1950-53

BOTH: WIDE WORLD

informed of much of anything.

On July 24, after one of the sessions of the Potsdam Conference, Truman got up from the baize-covered table and sauntered around to Stalin. The President had left his interpreter, Charles Bohlen, behind and relied on Stalin's personal translator—signifying that he had nothing important to say, just idle, end-of-the-day chit-chat.

"I was perhaps five yards away," Churchill recalled, "and I watched with the closest attention the momentous talk. I knew what the President was going to do. What was vital to measure was its effect on Stalin. I can see it all as if it were yesterday."

"I casually mentioned to Stalin," Truman wrote in his memoirs, "that we had a new weapon of unusual destructive force. The Russian Premier showed no special interest. All he said was that he was glad to hear it and hoped we would make 'good use of it against the Japanese.' "

"I was sure," Churchill said, "that [Stalin] had no idea of the significance of what he was being told . . . his face remained gay and genial and the talk between these two potentates soon came to an end. As we were waiting for our cars I found myself near Truman. 'How did it go?' I asked. 'He never asked a question,' he replied."

According to the Russian General Shtemenko, the ploy worked: the Russian Army staff "received no special instructions" after this meeting. According to Marshal Georgi K. Zhukov, commander of the Russian zone of occupation in Germany, Stalin returned from the meeting and told Molotov about Truman's remarks. Molotov "reacted immediately: 'Let them. We'll have to talk it over with Kurchatov and get him to speed things up.' I realized they were talking about research on the atomic bomb."

Whatever the case, whether Stalin realized what he had been told at the time, or only in retrospect, the nuclear arms race began, in effect, at Potsdam, on July 24, 1945, at 7:30 P.M.

Distrust, suspicion, anxiety, fear—all were intensified at Potsdam, and to them were added harshness and provocation, from all sides. During the next few months the agreements that had been reached were violated, or used as the bases for accusations of duplicity and bad faith. Many of the questions raised at Potsdam had been postponed and delegated to a Council of Foreign Ministers that was established to deal with these questions, and new ones, as they arose. The first meeting of the council was set for September, 1945. James Byrnes, before he left Washington to attend the meeting, had chatted with Secretary of War Henry Stimson. "I found that Byrnes was very much against any attempt to cooperate with Russia," Stimson noted in his diary. "His mind is full of his problems with the coming meeting of foreign ministers and he looks to have the presence of the bomb in his pocket, so to speak, as a great weapon to get through the thing. . . ." The British Chancellor of the Exchequer, Rt. Hon. Hugh Dalton, asked Foreign Minister Ernest Bevin how things were going, once the meeting started. "Like the strike leader said," Bevin replied, "thank God there is no danger of a settlement."

Not everyone was so quick or so eager to encourage the start of the Cold War. Henry Stimson was very much the elder statesman in 1945; he had spent more than fifty years in assorted government positions, and he foresaw dread consequences in Truman's developing policies toward Russia. Stimson had long thought that America should be tough with the Soviet Union, but he now believed that toughness was turning into harshness and harshness into provocativeness. In a memo that he wrote Truman in the autumn of 1945, he focused his thoughts around one of the most vexing problems of the postwar world:

". . . I consider the problem of our satisfactory relations with Russia as not merely connected with but as virtually dominated by the problem of the atomic bomb. Except for the problem of the control of that bomb, those relations, while vitally important, might not be immediately pressing. . . . But with the discovery of the bomb, they became immediately emergent. These relations may be perhaps irretrievably embittered by the way in which we approach the solution of the bomb with Russia. For if we fail to approach them now and merely continue to negotiate with them, having this weapon rather ostentatiously on our hip, their suspicions and their distrust of our purposes and motives will increase. . . .

"The chief lesson I have learned in a long life is that the only way you can make a man trustworthy is to trust him; and the surest way to make him untrustworthy is to distrust him and show your distrust."

Men like Stimson—and Henry Wallace, then Secretary of Commerce—were allowed, or forced, to resign. Others, those who tended to believe in an aggressive attitude toward Russia, were spotted, and promoted—young men such as John Foster Dulles and Dean Rusk. George Kennan, then in the American embassy in Moscow, was discovered after he sent a perfervid 8,000-word cable back to Washington: "We have here a political force committed fanatically to the belief that with U.S. there can be no permanent modus vivendi, that it is desirable and necessary that the internal harmony of our society be disrupted, our traditional way of life be destroyed, the international authority of our state be broken. . . ." In his memoirs, Kennan says that he now looks back on his cable "with horrified amusement." At the time, however, he was ideal for Truman's use, and he was recalled from Moscow and made chairman of the State Department's Policy

Senator Joseph R. McCarthy, 1950–54
U.P.I.

Opposite: funeral of Joseph Stalin, 1953
WIDE WORLD

Planning Committee, or as the *New York Times* called him, "America's global planner."

At Potsdam, the Big Three had all agreed to remove their troops from Iran. They set a deadline of March 2, 1946, and, as the deadline approached, the British announced that they would be leaving. The Russians, however, let it be known that they were somewhat reluctant to leave until they had made an agreement with the Iranians for an oil concession, and, regardless even of that agreement, Stalin rather thought he would like to withdraw only from central Iran and keep some troops in northern Iran. Not all these matters were immediately clarified and so, on March 1, 1946, Stalin announced that Russian soldiers would remain in Iran "pending clarification of the situation."

President Truman, meanwhile, invited Winston Churchill to deliver an address in March, 1946, at Fulton, Missouri: "A shadow has fallen upon the scenes so lately lighted by the Allied victory," said the former prime minister. "Nobody knows what Soviet Russia and its Communist international organization intends to do in the immediate future, or what are the limits, if any, to their expansive and proselytising tendencies.... From Stettin in the Baltic to Trieste in the Adriatic [the line, as Churchill neglected to mention, to which he and Truman had agreed at Potsdam], an iron curtain has descended across the Continent. Behind that line lie all the capitals of the ancient states of Central and Eastern Europe... in what I must call the Soviet sphere.... this is certainly not the Liberated Europe we fought to build up. Nor is it one which contains the essentials of permanent peace."

In Moscow, a well-rehearsed Russian reporter quizzed Stalin.

QUESTION: "How do you appraise Mr. Churchill's latest speech in the United States?"

STALIN: "I appraise it as a dangerous act, calculated to sow the seeds of dissension among the Allied states and impede their collaboration."

QUESTION: "Can it be considered that Mr. Churchill's speech is prejudicial to the cause of peace and security?"

STALIN: "Yes, unquestionably. As a matter of fact, Mr. Churchill now takes the stand of the warmongers, and in this Mr. Churchill is not alone. He has friends not only in Britain but in the United States of America as well."

During the winter of 1946-47, a succession of snowstorms hit Britain. Coal was already in short supply; factories had already closed for lack of fuel that winter. With the blizzards came rationing, first of electricity and then of food; finally heat was cut off. Britain, as Louis Halle wrote, "was like a soldier wounded in war who, now that fighting was over, was bleeding to death." The empire was at last dying.

In Washington, on February 21, 1947, a Friday afternoon, First Secretary H. M. Sichel of the British embassy delivered two notes to Loy Henderson at the State Department. Until that moment, Britain had been the principal support for the economy of Greece and the provider for the Turkish Army. The first of Sichel's notes said that Britain could no longer support Greece; the second said Britain could no longer underwrite the Turkish Army. "What the two notes reported," Halle observed, "was the final end of the *Pax Britannica*."

The following week, on February 27, Truman met with congressional leaders in the White House. Undersecretary of State Dean Acheson was present at the meeting, and Truman had him tell the congressmen what was at stake. Acheson spoke for ten minutes, informing the legislators that nothing less than the survival of the whole of Western civilization was in the balance at that moment; he worked in references to ancient Athens, Rome, and the course of Western civilization and freedoms since those times. The congressmen were silent for a few moments, and then, at last, Senator Arthur Vandenberg of Michigan, a prominent Republican who had come to support an active foreign policy, spoke up. All this might be true, Vandenberg said; but, if the President wished to sell his program to the American people, he would have to "scare hell out of the country." It was at that moment that the Cold War began in earnest for the United States.

It would be nice to be able to say that one nation held back from the nattering and abusiveness, that one seemed reluctant to start a conflict with its former allies, that one tried to compose the differences that had predictably arisen at the end of the war, that this one was the first to make a provocative move or charge and that one was last—but in truth all three leaped into the fray with such haste and determination that the origins of the Cold War are lost in a blur of all three sides hastening to be first in battle.

It is difficult to know the effects the Cold War had upon the Russian people in these years. But America paid heavy costs. When a nation has an actively internationalist, interventionist foreign policy, political power in that country tends to flow to the central government, and, within the central government, to the executive branch. That there was, in recent times, the creation of an "imperial presidency" in the U.S. was no quirk or happenstance; it was the natural outgrowth of the Cold War. From the imperial presidency, from the disorientation of the constitutional system of checks and balances, Watergate, proteiform and proliferating spy organizations, the impotence and decadence of Congress—all these were almost inevitable. That is why George Washington, a profoundly sophisticated man, advised Americans to avoid foreign entanglements; and that is why Americans who prize their freedom have always been a peace-loving people.

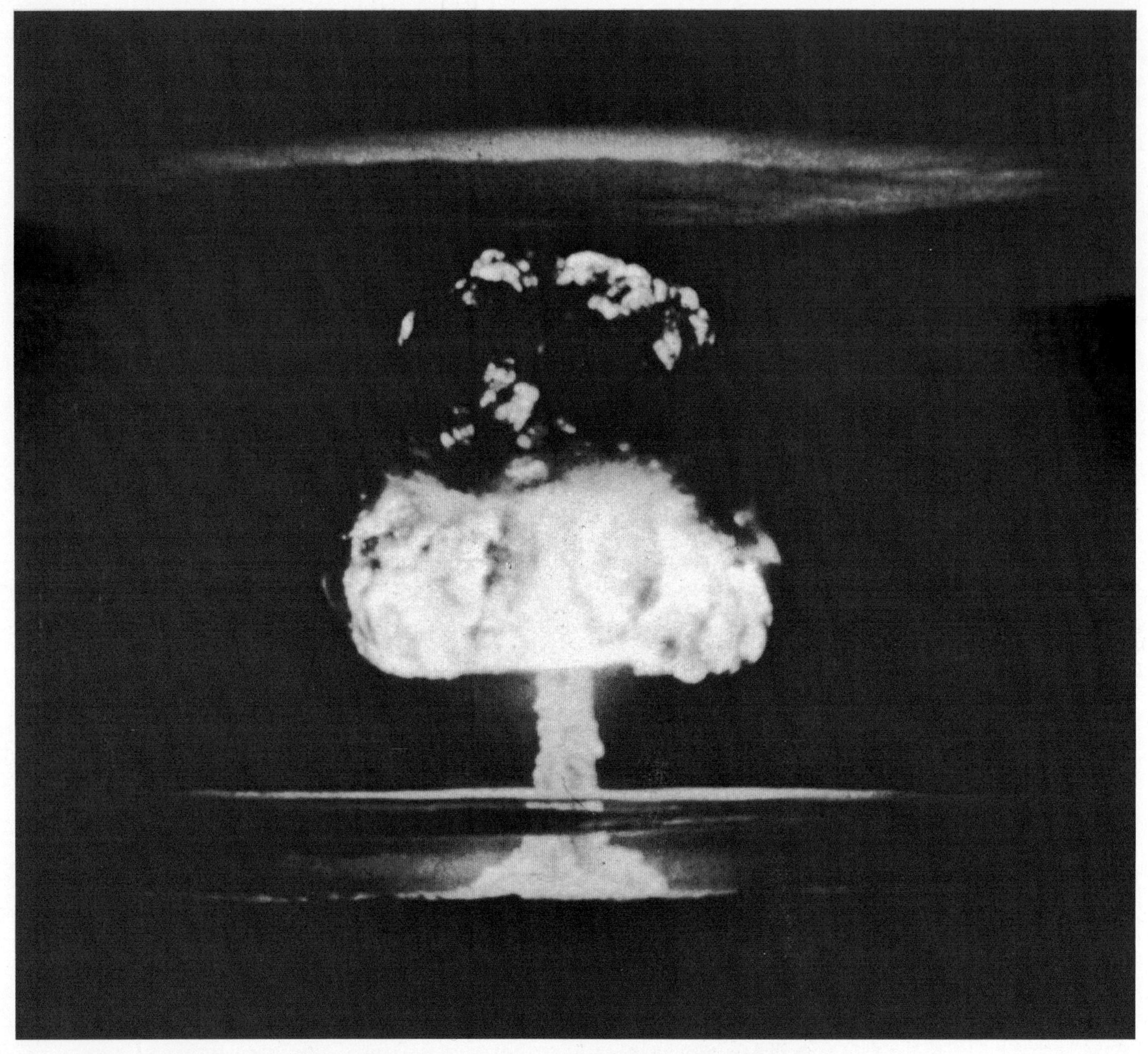

2. "We Can't Do Business With Stalin"

by W. Averell Harriman and Elie Abel

Even at this late date it is far from clear that the Cold War in Europe could have been avoided, once the certainty of Hitler's defeat had robbed the wartime alliance of its compelling necessity. The revisionist notion that Harry Truman, beguiled by the wrong set of advisers and emboldened by the success of the atomic bomb, started the Cold War by setting out to reverse Franklin Roosevelt's policies of wartime cooperation with the Soviet Union has been all too widely accepted. No one can say with assurance how Roosevelt would have dealt with the postwar challenge had he lived to serve out his fourth term. But there is persuasive evidence that in the last weeks of his life, after his return from the Yalta Conference, Roosevelt had substantially lost confidence in Stalin's word. He said as much to Anna Rosenberg (Hoffman) on March 23, 1945, less than three weeks before his death at Warm Springs. "We can't do business with Stalin," the President exclaimed. "He has broken every one of the promises he made at Yalta." To Anne O'Hare McCormick, another old friend, Roosevelt said that he now realized Stalin was not a man of his word; either that or he was no longer in control of the Soviet government.

The record of Roosevelt's messages to Stalin and Churchill in the final weeks of his life traces a rising curve of disappointment and frustration, together with the first sign of a new readiness to consider harder policies toward the Soviet Union.

From the perspective of Spaso House, Ambassador Harriman's residence in Moscow, a definite change of atmosphere could be felt many months before Roosevelt's death, indeed before Yalta. The war had been going well in the summer of 1944. General Eisenhower's forces made good their landing in Normandy. The Red Army was driving the German invaders from Soviet soil. There could be no question that final victory would be ours in a matter of months. On June 10, four days after D-Day in France, Stalin at last acknowledged the tremendous achievement of American and British arms in crossing the English Channel to attack Hitler's European Fortress from the west. Stalin's bitter reproaches of 1942 and 1943 ("The British are too cowardly to fight") were forgotten. "The history of war," he said to the American ambassador, "has never witnessed such a grandiose operation. Napoleon himself never attempted it. Hitler envisaged it but he was a fool for never having attempted it."

Six weeks later, as the Red Army rolled westward into Poland, fighting for the first time on foreign territory, Stalin broke a promise to Roosevelt. Acting without consultation or warning to his allies, he assigned "full responsibility in matters of civil government" on Polish territory to a newly formed Polish Committee for National Liberation (soon to be known as the Lublin Committee). The Polish government, which had taken refuge in London after the German invasion in 1939, abruptly found itself confronted with a rival regime, one already installed on Polish soil and enjoying the powerful support of the Soviet Union. The American embassy in Moscow had long since warned Roosevelt and his Secretary of State, Cordell Hull, against just such a *fait accompli*. As early as March 3, 1944, Stalin had shown his hand in a conversation with the American ambassador. "While the Red Army is liberating Poland," he said, "[Stanislaw] Mikolajczyk [premier of the Polish government in exile] will go on repeating his platitudes. By the time Poland is liberated, Mikolajczyk's Government will have changed, or another government will have emerged in Poland."

Poland had become the touchstone of Soviet behavior after the war was won, the first test of Stalin's attitude toward his weaker neighbors to the west. From Spaso House, all the brave talk about a free, independent Poland emerging from the war came to sound more and more improbable. Cordell Hull was not disposed to listen when the ambassador urged upon him the supreme importance of pressing the London Poles to come to terms with the Kremlin before the Red Army took matters into its hands. Roosevelt preferred to leave the prickly Polish problem to the British. He faced a tough campaign for re-election. The last thing he wanted was to involve himself in the delicate questions of Poland's postwar boundaries or the reconstruction of the London exile government to make it more palatable to the Russians. He feared the wrath of Polish-American voters in Buffalo, Hamtramck, and Chicago.

But events inside Poland would not wait. On July 23, the Red Army captured Lublin. Brest-Litovsk fell on July 26. Three days later the right flank of Marshal Rokossovsky's First White Russian Front reached the east bank of the river Vistula, opposite Warsaw. When the reluctant Mikolajczyk at last flew to Moscow and saw Stalin on August 3, the city had risen up in arms against the Germans. "Warsaw will be free any day," Mikolajczyk said. "God grant that it be so," Stalin responded. But when the Polish leader asked for Soviet help to the embattled city, Stalin sneered at the weakness of the so-called Home Army: "What kind of army is it—without artillery, tanks, air force? They do not even have enough hand weapons. In modern war this is nothing . . . ." Stalin added that he would supply no arms to the uprising. "For this reason," he said, tightening the screw on the London Poles, "you have to reach an understanding with the Lublin Committee. . . . We cannot tolerate two [Polish] governments."

Warsaw's agony was to last sixty-two days. While the Home Army fought a doomed battle in the streets against heavily reinforced German divisions, Stalin refused any help. Marshal Rokossovsky, who had outrun his supply lines, needed more time to attempt a crossing of the Vistula. Roosevelt and Churchill appealed repeatedly for Soviet cooperation with the Allied air forces in dropping arms and supplies to the Warsaw street fighters—to no avail. On August 16, Andrei Vishinsky, Stalin's deputy foreign minister, rejected one more plea from the British and American ambassadors. The Soviet government, Vishinsky said, "does not wish to associate itself, directly or indirectly, with the adventure in Warsaw."

Not until September 9 did Stalin agree to go along with the Allied plan for air drops of supplies by allowing U.S. and British bombers to land and refuel at American bases in the Ukraine. By that time the battle of Warsaw was all but lost. The defense perimeter had been broken by German tanks. Most of the arms and supplies fell beyond reach of the Polish insurgents. When the exhausted remnant of the Home Army at last laid down its arms on October 2, nearly a quarter million Poles were dead. Stalin's indifference was bound to shock his western allies and to persuade millions round the world that it suited his purpose to see anti-Communist Poles slaughtered by the Germans. They would not be around after the war to challenge the rule of his chosen instrument, the Lublin Committee.

Opposite: H-bomb test, Bikini Island, 1954
ENERGY RESEARCH AND DEVELOPMENT ADMINISTRATION

Roosevelt was no less affected by the tragedy of Warsaw than was his embassy in Moscow. His belief in the good intentions of Stalin had been damaged. In a discussion with the visiting ambassador to the Soviet Union on November 10, Roosevelt listened gravely to an account of Stalin's plan to join the war against Japan by attacking Manchuria and driving into northern China. The question in his mind, the President said, was "If the Russians go in, will they ever go out?" It was a question he had not raised in the case of eastern Europe, perhaps because he knew the answer. Through the autumn and winter of 1944-45, however, Roosevelt clung to his policy of postponing territorial settlements until the war was over. When the London Poles asked for American guarantees of the new frontiers they were being pressed by Churchill and Stalin to accept, the President declined.

On November 24, Mikolajczyk resigned. America's refusal to endorse his claims, together with Churchill's unceasing pressure and the adamant refusal of the London Polish Cabinet to consider any change of Poland's prewar boundaries, left him no decent alternative.

The fate of Poland, in short, had been pretty much decided before Roosevelt and Churchill went to Yalta in February, 1945. Events were in the saddle with Stalin's troops in full control of the country, although they did not enter Warsaw until three months after the uprising had been crushed. The Lublin Committee, now transformed into the Provisional Government, was issuing decrees and seeing them carried out. Its legitimacy continued to be questioned in London and Washington. But it would have taken a great deal more leverage than Roosevelt and Churchill possessed, or could reasonably be expected to apply, in order to alter the fundamental situation. The Russians had the double advantage of proximity and power.

Stalin preferred weak neighbors. He wanted to make certain that they would never again serve as a pathway for German aggression. It is less clear that he intended to communize them, at least in the beginning. The fact that the Red Army was not welcomed as a liberating force when it entered Poland or Rumania must have shocked him. The bulk of the populations remained sullen and antagonistic, as many are to this day. Stalin had agreed to free elections at Yalta, but he soon discovered that he dared not risk a free choice at the ballot box. In time he came to believe that the only way to assure himself of reasonably friendly neighboring governments in eastern Europe was to promote the establishment of Communist-dominated regimes beholden to Russia.

In Rumania, the detailed story was different but the outcome much the same. Here King Michael had courageously dismissed the pro-German government of Marshal Ion Antonescu in the summer of 1944 and offered to join forces with the Soviet Union. An Allied Control Commission, clearly subordinate to the Soviet high command, was set up in Bucharest to supervise the armistice. The U.S. representative, Brigadier General Cortland T. Van Rennselaer Schuyler, found himself free to observe, to complain, and to report back to his government in Washington. But his complaints were ignored by the Soviet representative.

The first postwar government in Bucharest, headed by General Nicolae Radescu, had been a coalition of noncommunist and communist parties. In a prophetic telegram dated February 20, 1945, General Schuyler warned that the Russians were determined to disintegrate the country's historic noncommunist parties by creating a situation in which only a government of the Left could maintain order. Four days later the National Democratic Front, organized and led by the Communists, staged a mass demonstration in Bucharest. When police fired a burst over the heads of the crowd, the Communists accused Radescu's coalition of creating a "massacre." They demanded Radescu's dismissal. When King Michael hesitated, Vishinsky flew in from Moscow to serve an ultimatum. The king, he said, had "just two hours and five minutes to inform the public that General Radescu has been dismissed."

The United States and Britain protested, reminding the Russians of their obligations under the Atlantic Charter, the Yalta agreements, and the Rumanian armistice agreement to consult their allies and to maintain a broadly representative government, pending the promised free election. But by nightfall of March 6, the king saw no alternative other than submission. He dismissed Radescu and named Petru Groza, the Soviet choice, as premier of a new Coalition Cabinet, one thoroughly obedient to the will of the Russians. Here again Soviet proximity and power had prevailed.

Debarred from more forceful action, Washington and London refused to recognize the Groza regime. Roosevelt was fully aware that the overwhelming power at his command did not reach to Bucharest. On March 11, he wrote to Churchill:

"I am fully determined, as I know you are, not to let the good decisions we reached at the Crimea slip through our hands and will certainly do everything I can to hold Stalin to their honest fulfillment. In regard to the Rumanian situation, Averell [Harriman] has taken up and is taking up again the whole question with Molotov, invoking the [Yalta] Declaration on Liberated Europe, and has proposed tripartite discussions to carry out these responsibilities. It is obvious that the Russians have installed a minority government of their own choosing, but . . . Rumania is not a good place for a test case. The Russians have been in undisputed

Hungarian Revolution, 1956
WIDE WORLD

Nikita Khrushchev at the U.N., 1960
U.P.I.

control from the beginning and with Rumania lying athwart the Russian lines of communications it is more difficult to contest the plea of military necessity and security which they are using to justify their action. We shall certainly do everything we can, however, and of course will count on your support."

It seems pointless, therefore, to blame Roosevelt for entering into agreements that "gave Stalin almost complete control of the internal affairs of the ex-Nazi satellites in eastern Europe." The gift was not his to make.

Imminent victory had other corrosive effects upon the wartime alliance. No single incident of the dozens that could be cited makes this point more eloquently than the falling out between Roosevelt and Stalin over the unfulfilled possibility of a German surrender to the Western Allies in northern Italy. Karl Wolff, the ranking S.S. officer in Italy, had approached Allen W. Dulles, then the Berne chief of the Office of Strategic Services, to explore terms for ending German resistance on that front. Dulles told Wolff there could be no negotiation over terms; the Allies would insist on unconditional surrender. When the American ambassador notified the Soviet government of this development on March 12, 1945, Molotov raised no objection. He asked only that Soviet officers be allowed to take part in the talks. Since the Russians had no diplomatic relations with neutral Switzerland, he hoped the United States would intercede to make possible their participation in any future talks on Swiss soil.

The Combined Chiefs of Staff in Washington objected that the only purpose of the Berne contacts was to arrange for the appearance of German representatives at Allied headquarters in Caserta, Italy, where the Soviets could participate with no difficulty. Molotov furiously insisted that the contacts at Berne be broken off at once. There could be no surrender talks, he insisted, without Soviet participation.

Roosevelt promptly sent a message to Stalin, carefully explaining how the German overture was being handled and assuring the Russians that no deal would be concluded behind their backs. Stalin countered with a bitter accusation that the Germans were "opening their front to the Anglo-American troops in Italy" for an evil purpose—so they could shift troops to the east and concentrate their fire on the Red Army.

With scrupulous forebearance, Roosevelt replied that no surrender negotiations had been entered into; the Berne meeting had been solely for the purpose of arranging contact with competent German officers, and it had been fruitless; Soviet representatives could take part in future negotiations at Caserta, if any; and there could be no question of allowing the Germans to shift troops to the Eastern Front.

Stalin brusquely rejected Roosevelt's careful explanation:

"You insist that there have been no negotiations yet.

"It may be assumed that you have not been fully informed. As regards my military colleagues, they, on the basis of data which they have on hand, do not have any doubts that the negotiations have taken place and that they have ended in an agreement with the Germans, on the basis of which the German commander on the western front, Marshal Kesselring, has agreed to open the front and permit the Anglo-American troops to advance to the east and the Anglo-Americans have promised in return to ease for the Germans the peace terms.

"I think that my colleagues are close to the truth. . . ."

Roosevelt was thunderstruck by this accusation. He had trusted Stalin; he expected to be trusted in return. Instead, he was now accused of betraying an ally, of being in league with the Nazis, and of being a liar or dupe as well. For the first time, in reply, he allowed his feelings to show:

". . . It would be one of the great tragedies of history if at the very moment of the victory, now within our grasp, such distrust, such lack of faith, should prejudice the entire undertaking after the colossal losses of life, material and treasure involved.

"Frankly I cannot avoid a feeling of bitter resentment toward your informers, whoever they are, for such vile misrepresentations of my actions or those of my trusted subordinates."

Nothing more, in fact, came of the Italian surrender talks. When General Wolff, after a mystifying delay, asked for various assurances that went beyond the simple unconditional surrender formula, the Allied commander in Italy, Field Marshal Sir Harold Alexander, flatly refused.

President Roosevelt, however, was deeply affected by the incident. He had never been so grossly insulted throughout his long correspondence over the war years with Stalin. His progressive disenchantment had been tempered by an inexhaustible optimism that the new postwar world would be a cleaner, better place thanks to his brain child, the United Nations. Now, in the final weeks of his life, Roosevelt had been jarred into a painful recognition that in the years to come the world might be a far more difficult, dangerous place than he had allowed himself to believe till then. "We must be firm," he wrote to Churchill on April 12, from Warm Springs. On the same day, he cabled the ambassador in Moscow: ". . . it is my desire to consider the Berne misunderstanding a minor incident."

Even if Roosevelt had not died that day, the imminent collapse of Hitler's war machine was bound to alter the political calculus within the alliance. As the Nazi threat diminished, so did the need for Allied cooperation. Russia fought no longer for survival but for long-term security and great power recognition. A free hand in eastern Europe was, by Stalin's reckoning, no less than his due.

Once before, in 1941, he had offered the British a sphere-of-influence agreement: Britain would formally recognize Soviet absorption of the Baltic states, part of Finland, eastern Poland, and Bessarabia, in exchange for Russian support of British bases and security arrangements in western Europe. Mindful that Roosevelt and Hull would reject such a deal, Churchill had said no.

Three years later, however, the prime minister, while in Moscow, offered Stalin a more ambitious sphere-of-influence arrangement. Russia could have "ninety per cent preponderance" in Rumania, a 75-25 split in Bulgaria, plus a fifty-fifty split in Yugoslavia and Hungary in exchange for Britain's "ninety per cent of the say" in Greece. Stalin penciled a blue check on the sheet of paper that Churchill had pushed across the table to him. But both men were fully aware that Roosevelt would frown on such arrangements. The President had sent Stalin a message on October 4, 1944, making clear that he would not be bound by any bilateral bargains struck in his absence:

"I am sure you understand that in this global war there is literally no question, military or political, in which the United States is not interested. I am firmly convinced that the three of us, and only the three of us, can find the solution of the questions still unresolved."

Roosevelt expanded on his misgivings in a message the same day to his ambassador:

"Quite frankly, I can tell you, but only for you and not to be communicated under any circumstances to the British or the Russians, that I would have preferred very much to have the next conference between the three of us for the very reasons stated to Marshal Stalin. . . . Therefore you should bear in mind that there are no subjects of discussion that I can anticipate between Marshal Stalin and the Prime Minister in which I will not be greatly interested. Consequently it is of importance that Mr. Hull and I have complete freedom of action when this conference is over."

The ambassador followed his instructions faithfully. When Churchill on October 12 showed him the draft of a letter to Stalin setting down for the record the British interpretation of the percentages arrangement so casually agreed to three days earlier, the ambassador warned that Roosevelt and Hull would certainly repudiate it. Churchill decided against delivering his letter to Stalin and the matter was never again raised among the Big Three. In short, the episode offers the historian little more than "an authentic account" of Churchill's thoughts at the time, as the prime minister himself described it in his war memoirs.

Too much can be made of such scraps of paper. Mr. Mee does just that in his treatment of the Potsdam Conference session on August 1, 1945. Seizing upon what purports to be a Soviet transcript of that meeting, he reproduces an exchange among Stalin, Truman, and Clement Attlee, the new British prime minister, with their respective foreign ministers, on the question of reparations to be paid by Germany in defeat. This exchange, dealing specifically with German assets and how they were to be divided among the Allies, has been wrenched from its context and made to bear more weight than it can possibly sustain. It was not, in fact, a discussion of spheres of interest or any kind of deal to carve up the map of Europe. It needs to be seen for no more than what it is—a discussion of German assets in foreign countries and how they were to be disposed of, all this within the wider context of an Allied agreement on the reparations to be exacted from Germany.

Mr. Mee goes on to express astonishment that Germany should somehow have emerged as the "very center and source" of the Cold War as a result of the Potsdam negotiations. Surely the stubborn facts of history and geography had established Germany's central position in European policy calculations long before Potsdam. Here was the most powerful, energetic nation in the very heart of Europe brought low by the combined forces of Russia, Britain, and the United States. One can quarrel with certain of the Potsdam decisions for dealing with Germany after the war. But it is hard to see how the centrality of Germany in the European landscape could have been waved away by an alternative set of decisions.

Mr. Mee has made his own sketchy revision of standard revisionist doctrine. He parts company with the first generation of revisionist writers by spreading the Cold War guilt around, instead of fastening on President Truman as the archvillain. The Cold War, he now argues, served everybody's purpose. Stalin "needed the Cold War . . . to discipline his restless people at home." Churchill needed it because the only hope he saw of preserving some measure of British influence in world affairs was to set—and to keep—America and Russia at one another's throats. But Truman still gets the worst of the argument. He is accused of "institutionalizing" the Cold War in order to maintain prosperity at home. Truman needed an excuse for deficit spending, so the Mee theory goes, because without it he could not have kept the American economy busy and productive. Thus he waged a Cold War, after the hot war was won, to justify continued deficit spending. "Eventually," as Mee would have it, "with the Truman Doctrine and the Marshall Plan, the encouragement of American multinational companies, and a set of defense treaties that came finally to encompass the world, he institutionalized it."

An ugly accusation, this, which stands certain durable facts on their heads. There is the fact, for example, that Truman demobi-

Cuban Missile Crisis, 1962
WIDE WORLD

Opposite: Vietnam, 1963–75
U.S. MARINE CORPS

lized the Army and Navy with extraordinary speed as soon as World War II was won. From a combined strength of twelve million in 1945, he cut back the armed services to fewer than 1,600,000 men in 1947. By 1949 the Army was down to ten divisions. Between 1947 and 1950 he kept the national defense budget to an average of $13 billion a year. These are hardly the actions of a President determined to throw his weight around and to maintain prosperity through forced deficit spending.

It is not clear from Mee's narrative what part, if any, the encouragement of American multinational companies could have played in this development. Precious few American companies were doing business in Europe thirty years ago. Precious little business of any kind was being transacted in the wasteland of broken stone and brick to which many of the great metropolitan centers of Europe had been reduced. Transportation and power grids were shattered; coal and industrial raw materials were in short supply; black markets flourished everywhere; food commanded a king's ransom in the wildly inflated currencies of postwar Europe. Would Mr. Mee have refused to assist in restoring and rebuilding Europe for the sake of a balanced budget? It is not an unfair question. Obviously there were other, more honorable, motives at work than a presidential preference for deficit spending.

As for the Truman Doctrine, the Marshall Plan—and NATO—these were beyond question Truman's accomplishments. Not, however, the "set of defense treaties that came finally to encompass the world." The major responsibility for Seato, the Baghdad Pact, and the rest properly belongs to John Foster Dulles.

Having disposed of eastern Europe and Germany, Mr. Mee then turns to the atomic bomb. Here again Truman is portrayed as the villain of the peace. "In obstinate defiance of all other opinion," we are told, Truman insisted that dropping the bomb on Japan was militarily necessary.

The few opinions Mee cites against the argument of military necessity are for the most part regrettably retrospective: the Strategic Bombing Survey, for example, which concluded *after* the war that Japan would have surrendered even if the Hiroshima and Nagasaki bombs had not been dropped. That Japan would have surrendered eventually is not disputed here. The unanswered question was *when* that might happen—and how many months longer the war in the Pacific might drag on if the bomb was not dropped. We know today that Japanese counsels were divided on whether or not to end the fighting. Even after Hiroshima, the Japanese military chiefs vetoed an effort by influential civilians to accept the Potsdam Proclamation calling for unconditional surrender. Even after the second bomb had fallen, on Nagasaki, the military persisted in their refusal to surrender. It took the personal intervention of Emperor Hirohito to overcome that entrenched opposition.

The plain fact, however, is that Truman had no knowledge of these goings-on. A month before the Alamogordo test, he had received from General Marshall and approved a military plan for the invasion of the Japanese home islands. The American Sixth Army was to land on Kyushu about November 1. Four months later there would be a second invasion, the Eighth and Tenth armies going ashore on Honshu. Marshall expected fierce resistance with the loss of a half-million Americans. He speculated that the Japanese would not be brought to their knees until late autumn, 1946.

After Alamogordo, with Truman and his Joint Chiefs still at Potsdam, the decision was made to drop the bomb in the belief that its use would rule out the need to invade Japan—and would save the lives of hundreds of thousands of GI's. Right or wrong, there is no persuasive evidence that the decision was challenged or questioned at the time. Churchill recalls in his memoirs: "The historic fact remains, and must be judged in the after-time, that the decision whether or not to use the atomic bomb to compel the surrender of Japan was never even an issue. There was unanimous, automatic, unquestioned agreement around our table; nor did I ever hear the slightest suggestion that we should do otherwise." Even Stalin, when Truman informed him of the Alamogordo test on July 24 at Potsdam, expressed the hope that the United States would "make good use" of the new weapon against Japan. It would appear that Mr. Mee has left out of his account several opinions that do not fit his thesis.

It is not the purpose of the authors to defend Roosevelt and Truman against all findings of faulty judgment. The elusive truth will not be pinned down, however, by substantially ignoring the context in which many of the difficult wartime decisions were necessarily taken. In simple justice to President Truman, it is worth noting that as late as 1948, when Stalin closed off Allied access to Berlin, the President never threatened the Russians with atomic bombs, although the American monopoly was still intact. Instead he chose the least provocative response—an airlift of essential supplies to the beleaguered city.

Roosevelt or Truman, Stalin, Churchill or Attlee—all labored under a common handicap when compared with contemporary historians: they lacked the benefits of hindsight. Mee contends that they also shared a vested interest in maintaining international tension. He imputes to them the deliberate choice of increasing tension, even at the risk of a third world war, because that course promised various benefits to the peoples of their respective countries. To believe that is to deny these men their humanity.

3. Mr. Mee Replies

Mr. Abel and Ambassador Harriman may well be right in their understanding of the origins of the Cold War. I believe they are right in most of what they say in the first half of their comments, and, on some issues, I think they are making points that I was trying to make myself. For example, that the "fate of Poland . . . had been pretty much decided before Roosevelt and Churchill went to Yalta in February, 1945" is one thing I was attempting to express; that "as the Nazi threat diminished, so did the need for Allied cooperation" is another.

On other points, I believe Mr. Abel and the ambassador are mistaken:

1) They say, "Seizing upon what purports to be a Soviet transcript of" the Potsdam plenary session of August 1, 1945, I reproduce an exchange among the Big Three that appears to outline explicitly understood spheres of interest in the world. I don't know what is meant by "purports." I have quoted what the Soviet government has published as its English-language version of the conference transcripts. Now, it is possible that the Soviets just made up this exchange out of whole cloth: they have been known to have a taste for inventing history. And it is true that the American notes, which are not literal transcripts, and which are often sketchier than the other countries' sets of transcripts, do not appear to cover such a specific discussion of global spheres of interest. But when we turn to the British records (to be found in the Foreign Office archives under file reference CAB 99 38 8461), they seem to confirm the Russian transcripts.

2) I go on, they observe, "to express astonishment that Germany should somehow have emerged as the 'very center and source' of the Cold War as a result of the Potsdam negotiations"; they imply that I have ignored Germany's historically central position in European policy calculations. But, no, of course Germany was in the same geographical neighborhood before Potsdam. That is not the issue I meant to raise. The issue is whether mere geographical position creates an inevitable *casus belli*. I think not. To believe that it does is to believe in a form of historical determinism.

3) They remark that "Truman demobilized the Army and Navy with extraordinary speed." Well, yes, he did. I am not sure that the point is entirely relevant, but the truth is that he could not do otherwise, given America's traditional aversion to standing armies and the climate of opinion at the time. However, he tried. On August 17, 1945, three days after the surrender of Japan, he announced that he would ask Congress to approve a program of Universal Military Training. Congress declined. Demobilization proceeded.

4) It is also true, as they point out, that Truman "kept the national defense budget to an average of $13 billion a year" between 1947 and 1950—but it is really not possible to slip by the context of that so easily. In 1939 the entire federal budget—covering all U.S. domestic and foreign operations, including all the programs of the New Deal—was $9 billion. During the war, it increased more than tenfold, to grotesque proportions by the standards of the day. Then, after the war, Truman held just the defense portion of the budget to $13 billion. For a peacetime budget, in that era, and just after Congress had quashed Universal Military Training, $13 billion was a fierce sum of money.

5) That, as they say, "precious few American companies were doing business in Europe thirty years ago" is a point I was trying to make; the multinational companies followed the Marshall Plan. A number of Frenchmen have written eloquently on the matter.

6) "The few opinions Mee cites against the argument of military necessity [for the use of the atomic bomb] are for the most part regrettably retrospective." This is not, regrettably, true. The Strategic Bombing Survey spoke *after* the war. But Eisenhower of the Army, Leahy and King of the Navy, LeMay and Arnold of the Air Force, and others told Truman *before* the bomb was used that it was not militarily necessary. That is the fact, whether or not it is persuasive.

The plan to use the atomic bomb in order to save an indeterminable number of American lives had been accepted long before Potsdam. But military situations change: that is the nature of war. And, in a changing military situation, a competent general changes his plans. To imagine that American military commanders would not change their plans in a fluid situation is to imagine that the American command was composed of obstinate fools. The notion is a beguiling one, I grant, but it does not seem to be true.

Indeed, as men such as Eisenhower and Leahy and LeMay saw the military situation in Japan change—as they observed that the Japanese were not able to get a single one of their planes off the ground by the time of Potsdam—they changed their minds about what was needed to end the war.

The military men were flexible; it was the diplomats, some of them (not Ambassador Harriman, I hasten to note) who were inflexible. Why? In this case, I can only suppose, in default of another plausible explanation, that it is at least marginally possible—however extraordinary—that the American Secretary of State told the truth when he said that the bomb was used not for military reasons but for the diplomatic aim of making "Russia more manageable in Europe."

7) Mr. Abel and Ambassador Harriman quote Churchill as saying that there was "unanimous, automatic, unquestioned agreement around our table" about the use of the bomb. The pertinent question this raises is what table Churchill sat around.

Finally, I am vexed about the relatively minor point that Mr. Abel and Ambassador Harriman still believe that Truman "informed" Stalin about the atomic bomb. As Churchill makes clear in his *Memoirs of the Second World War* (and Byrnes in his, Leahy in his, and Bohlen in his), Truman purposely told Stalin about the existence of "a new weapon of unusual destructive force" in a vague fashion precisely because he hoped Stalin would *not* understand that he was being told about an atomic bomb.

To believe that these men acted as I have suggested is not to deny them their humanity at all; quite the contrary: it is simply not to deny the possibility that they were human. ☆

Opposite: East German border guard peers over the Berlin Wall.
KLAUS MANN

ROUTE 66:

by Thomas W. Pew, Jr.

Ghost Road of the Okies

People who have been turned out of their homes make keen historians. Forced from the land of their ancestors and onto the open road without a destination, they have a way of remembering—often to the minute of the day—the trauma of departure. Etched indelibly in their memories are the details: a frenetic packing; a final, hurried look around an abandoned house; a wistful, wishful fondling of familiar possessions that couldn't be taken with them; then, if they were lucky and had wheels instead of just shoe leather and shoulders beneath their possessions, there was the wrenching moment of the last, silent, no-looks-back drive out to the nearest highway.

Five hundred thousand such refugees fled the Great Plains and rural South in the dust and depression years of the 1930's. Funneled down the farm roads of the Dakotas, Nebraska, Kansas, Missouri, Oklahoma, Mississippi, Texas, New Mexico, and Arkansas, many of them could only say that their destination was "West." They knew, or so it seemed in the choking dust, with the hungry eyes of undernourished children watching them, that things just couldn't be worse than they already were on the failing farms. All they knew of home—the earth itself—was being slowly destroyed by what seemed to be a monstrous conspiracy between the malevolent forces of nature and the bewildering economics of depression.

The worst of it—the Dust Bowl itself—lay in parts of five states: Kansas, Oklahoma, Colorado, New Mexico, and Texas. It included ninety counties of these five states: ninety-seven million acres, of which thirty-two million were under cultivation. Whole families and old clans who had settled the land in these places, often before statehood, were pushed from their homesteads as though they were just nuisance hillocks in a field that had never known any more horsepower than one mule. When they piled and strapped their things on the old patched-together flivvers, all that they had was the hope they knew as California—that, and sometimes enough money to buy the gas to get them there. They were "Okies," "Arkies," and "Texies" (in time all would be lumped together in California under the name "Okies") and the highway they traveled West was U.S. Route 66, the road of desperation described by John Steinbeck in *The Grapes of Wrath* as "the path of a people in flight, refugees from dust and shrinking land, from the thunder of tractors and shrinking ownership, from the desert's slow northward invasion, from the twisting winds that howl up out of Texas, from the floods that bring no richness to the land and steal what little richness there is there. From all of these the people are in flight, and they come into 66 from the tributary side roads, from the wagon tracks and the rutted country roads. 66 is the mother road, the road of flight."

The route, if not the "mother road" itself, had a respectable history even before it witnessed the flight of the Okies. Parts of its northern leg from Chicago to the mouth of the Missouri River followed the 1673 portage route of Père Jacques Marquette and Louis Jolliet in their exploration of the upper Mississippi River. That portion that crossed Missouri in a southwesterly direction to Fort Smith, Arkansas, went along the route of the ancient Osage Indian trail—and also paralleled the line of the first telegraph to penetrate the southwest territories, giving it for a long time the name of the "Wire Road." In 1849, during the height of the Gold Rush to California, Captain Randolph B. Marcy and Lieutenant James H. Simpson were ordered to "make, and report, a reconnaissance" of a route from Fort Smith to Santa Fe, New Mexico, "in direct reference to the future location of a national road. . . ." The Marcy-Simpson expedition proceeded southwest across the Indian territories of Oklahoma, through the panhandle of Texas, crossed the Pecos River at Anton Chico, and rolled into Santa Fe on June 28, 1849.

It was another eight years before the remaining section of the route was officially marked and laid out by the government. In 1857, Lieutenant Edward Fitzgerald Beale was authorized to survey a wagon route along the 35th parallel from Fort Defiance, some 180 miles southwest of Santa Fe, to the Colorado River and California. Beale's expedition was distinguished from the Marcy-Simpson expedition chiefly by his use of more than seventy Bactrian and dromedary camels imported from Egypt and Arabia in an experiment dear to the heart of Jefferson Davis, then Secretary of War. By the time the expedition reached the Colorado in the late summer of 1857, Beale's admiration of the beasts knew no bounds: "The harder the test they are put to, the more fully they seem to justify all that can be said of them. . . . I look forward to the day when every mail route across the continent will be conducted . . . with this economical and noble brute." He also declared that the route now completely marked and mapped would "inevitably become the great emigrant road to California."

Beale overestimated the permanence of the camels, but was closer to the mark in his second declaration. Over the next fifty years, the wagon road from Fort Smith to California would be one of the best traveled of all the overland routes. It was only to be expected, then, that when the automobile began to nose its way into the West, this venerable, well-marked road would play yet another role in the history of overland travel.

In the 1920's a "66 Association" grew up among the communities that had clustered along the route over the years, the idea being to promote a highway that bore a single number all the way from Lake Michigan to the Pacific Ocean. In 1926 the road received the official title of U.S. Route 66. Over the years, bits and pieces were gradually connected and paved, a grade lowered here, a pass cut there, a bridge erected somewhere else, and by 1932 the "national road" of Marcy, Simpson, and Beale was a national highway that reached across the land. The road, the mother road, began at the corner of Jackson Boulevard and Michigan Avenue in Chicago and ran 2,200 miles through three time zones and eight states before it dead-ended at the corner of Santa Monica Boulevard and Ocean Avenue in Santa Monica. They called it the Main Street of America.

The Route 66 of memory is gone now—or most of it. Over the past two decades the freeway called Interstate 40 has taken away its name and its number, as well as obliterating much of the old roadbed, bypassing most of its little towns, and leaving only isolated and poorly maintained stretches of the original highway. Recently, this writer and photographer Terrence Moore drove some four thousand miles of tributary roads and "unimproved" segments of what is left of Route 66. Beginning in eastern Oklahoma we followed, where we could, the old way into the lush valley land of California where the highway ended and the Okies settled. Along the way we stopped and talked to the migrants who actually made the trip in the 1930's, and to the people who ran the filling stations and little stores that served those in flight when they could afford it. What follows is their history.

Along the old sections of Route 66 that pass through the Dust Bowl counties of Oklahoma and through the panhandle of Texas, the hills and flats are green with trees and native grass now. The restored land, after forty years of rest and recuperation, has forgotten the spasm of drought and dust accompanied by plagues of bugs and periodic floods that expelled its bewildered tenants. But the old householders from this land—those who survived with their wits and lungs intact, and those who

ALL PHOTOGRAPHS BY TERRENCE MOORE

Chief
ASOLINE

WITH

ETHYL

(TRADE MARK)
REG. U.S. PATENT OFF.

BRAND OF
ANTI-KNOCK
COMPOUND

ETHYL GASOLINE
CORPORATION
NEW YORK, U.S.A.

3-41 MADE IN U·S·A

endured pulverizing poverty as "pea pickers" in California—cannot forget.

Mrs. Flossie Scott (formerly Flossie Haggard and mother of country-western singer Merle Haggard) is one of them. And she remembers. The Haggards stuck it out in Oklahoma longer than many of their neighbors and kin, but on Monday, July 15, 1935, "about eleven o'clock in the morning," they couldn't hold out any longer against the dust, repeated crop failures, and, finally, a fire. The 74-year-old Mrs. Haggard, who came to the Oklahoma Territory when she was four years old, tells her story and the parallel history of thousands of other Okies, Arkies, and Texies—in these words:

"In 1932 we were farming in McIntosh County, Oklahoma. We had dairy cows and hogs, and farmed cotton also. The downward trend in prices started in that year. I remember we sold several fat hogs for two cents a pound. They would be one dollar or more per pound today. We grew all our food except for such as sugar, coffee and flour. Sorghum cane provided some of our sweets.

"New clothes were few and far between. 1934 brought a drought, and crops failed almost one-hundred per cent. And on top of that disaster, we had a fire that year that destroyed our barn, car, and feed.

"We moved into the little town of Checotah where Mr. Haggard ran a service station through the winter and spring of 1935. In July, 1935, we loaded some necessary supplies onto a two-wheel trailer and our 1926 model Chevrolet which Jim had overhauled. We headed for California on Route 66, as many friends and relatives had already done. We had our groceries with us—home sugar-cured bacon in a lard can, potatoes, canned vegetables, and fruit. We camped at night and I cooked bread in a Dutch oven. The only place we didn't sleep out was in Albuquerque where we took a cabin and where I can remember bathing.

"My sister Flora and family had gone to California a year before, so she sent us forty dollars to pay our expenses on the trip. I know now it took a lot of nerve to start so poorly equipped, but the good Lord was with us and we made it in four days, but not without some problems on the highway."

In the middle of the desert, Mrs. Haggard recalls, the car broke down. "We were out of water, and just when I thought we weren't going to make it, I saw this boy coming down the highway on a bicycle. He was going all the way from Kentucky to Fresno. He shared a quart of water with us and helped us fix the car. Everybody'd been treating us like trash, and I told this boy, 'I'm glad to see there's still some decent folks left in this world.' "

Mrs. Haggard's memory from her own experience has a remarkable parallel in *The Grapes of Wrath* when Ma Joad says, "I'm learnin' one thing good. Learnin' it all a time, ever' day. If you're in trouble or hurt or need—go to poor people. They're the only one's that'll help—the only ones."

Outside Needles, California, the Haggards camped down by the Colorado during the day so they could make the final dash across the Mojave Desert in the cool of the night. Mrs. Haggard was sick, she remembers, and a filling station man warned that she wouldn't make it if they tried the desert run in the heat. When they got to the lush San Joaquin Valley, she says, "we found many of our friends living in shacks made of cardboard or anything that could make a shelter from the sun, and provide a place to call home. They were working people, they did anything they could find to do, mostly fruit-picking until cotton-picking time. Many lived principally on cull fruits that the growers rejected and which could be gotten without cost. My husband could pick five hundred pounds of cotton a day, but fortunately he never had to. We got a job on a dairy milking forty Holstein cows by hand."

The Haggards worked at that job for two months, but when the children started school they had to give it up. Jim Haggard found a job then at the Santa Fe Railroad shops and "was lucky again and got on at forty cents an hour." Next the Haggards succeeded in getting a refrigerator car on a lot to live in. The owner wanted "someone to cut windows and doors in it and make it livable," Mrs. Haggard recalls. "She offered us nine months rent to do this work. We needed a roof over our heads, so we gladly accepted her offer. We moved in on September 15, 1935. It was a difficult task, cutting through seven inches of steel, wood and insulation, after working a full day's work at a job. But when we finished it was a comfortable place to live." Mrs. Haggard "dug a place for a garden and canned the surplus." She even "went to the garbage dumps and picked up jars." Her calm, strong face and her still hands, never far from a Bible, show the pride and wisdom of her hard life, and she says she wouldn't take anything for the experiences she has had—"to see both sides." Like many Okies we talked to, she wants one to know that the Haggards "were never on welfare." They worked and they made it. Not without suffering. But they made it.

Another remembrance of Route 66 comes from Ralph Richardson and his wife, who run a general store on a remote section of old Route 66 that was by-passed by the freeway in 1962. They opened the store there, outside Montoya, New Mexico, in 1928 when there were still "trail" markers on the unpaved road. From the looks of the place today, not much has changed since. The Richardson store, with old-fashioned gas pumps out front and a picnic table off to the side, is dominated by the large potbelly stove in the center and the mirror-door ice box toward the back. It is the local post office, the local dry goods store, and the local kerosene lamp and tool supply. It used to be a butcher shop, shoe store, meeting place, and everything else to the ranchers and train crews from miles around. Richardson, who constantly dusts, rearranges, and surveys the stock on his dark wood shelves while he talks, remembers the people who came by his store in the 1930's as "carrying their own food and having nothing. They were just a bunch of poor people starved out, flooded out, heading to California, trying to find a place to start over. They'd been through hell. If they were broke when they were here they'd work at cleaning up, chopping wood, cutting weeds, digging ditches—any kind of work in order to move on towards California."

"Times were so bad," his wife added without looking at her husband, "that it was a kind of nightmare. Sometimes you don't want to remember. We lost one child and thought we'd lose another in those times. The government had bought out our cattle and started killing them. Paid us almost nothing. And then all the time trying to hang onto this place on the highway. I tell you at times I was near crazy with our problems," she breathes, the focus of the memory catching her voice, filling her eyes, and putting an abrupt end to the interview.

Another long-term, roadside witness-participant in the history of Route 66 is mining engineer Ed Edgerton. He has lived beside or near Route 66 since 1915 (long before it was Route 66), and in 1929 started the filling station and camp where he lives today on the Sitgreaves Pass near Oatman, Arizona. In fact, Edgerton surveyed the section of Route 66 that runs past his place. He remembers the Okies and Arkies as folks who would work for one dollar a day. "It made the gold miners in Oatman mad," he said, "and they told the Okies to work for more or get out. The miners would say to those Okies, 'Don't cut our wages or we'll cut your throat.' Those broke Okies used to come here," Edgerton remembers, "come up to my gas pumps and say to me: 'Mister, if you could just get

us a couple of gallons of gas we'll coast into Needles where we've got friends.' " He recalls the nights in the twenties and thirties when fifty cars or more were parked around his place with families camping out. "Sometimes they'd work around the place, but they were anxious to get to California," he says, "and a lot of them didn't know there was a desert between here and the real California. I let them know about what was ahead and what was behind. I had a big sign out there by the water: '8½ miles to Oatman, Arizona–biggest car cemetery in the U.S.' And over there by the edge of 66 I had another sign on a Cholla cactus that said: 'Carry Water or This is What You'll Look Like.' "

Edgerton says he used to give a lot of gas away, but he also used to trade for it. "I'd take a gun, spare tire, maybe, watches, rings–'come on, honey, give me that ring'–and I'd hold these things. Then those folks would get out to California, make a little money, and send me some money and I'd mail their things back to them. They even offered to leave the dog, the cat, and the canary for gas. I learned a lot of different things about human nature in those times," says Edgerton, who admits to being closer to ninety than to eighty. When asked to characterize the hundreds of Dust Bowl refugees he saw pass his place on Route 66, one word comes immediately to his lips: "Frightened they were, those people were frightened, and they came through here thinking they were headed for the promised land where they'd say 'everything's going to be all right.' I warned them about those ideas, but they went on and, well, they didn't find the promised land."

Paul Taylor, who with his photographer wife Dorothea Lange did the field research that led to the publication of *American Exodus: A Record of Human Erosion*, in 1939, described the economic forces behind the Dust Bowl migration in a 1938 speech: "At the close of the [First World] War, prices of cotton and of wheat collapsed, and with them, many thousands of rural families were shaken from their positions on the agricultural ladder. Farm owners lost the equities in their farms and became tenants; tenants were reduced to laborers, and farm laborers did what they could. This process, begun in the depression of the early twenties, was accelerated by the Depression of the early thirties. Then came drought and grasshoppers, and whole sections of the rural population already loosened by the accumulating forces of successive depressions were finally dislodged by a catastrophe of Nature." They were "scattered like the dust of their farms, literally blown out. And they trekked into California, these American whites, at the end of a long immigrant line of Chinese, Japanese, Koreans, Negroes, Hindustanis, Mexicans, Filipinos, to serve the crops and farmers of our state."

From the status of independent farmers, they had fallen to that of cheap labor, and Sacramento's Paul Westmoreland–or "Okie Paul," as he is known to radio listeners throughout central California–was one of them. He was a teen-ager when he made the first run out of Oklahoma with his family. "We was starved out in 1929," he recalls, "ahead of the *Grapes of Wrath* bunch. We went to Shamrock, Texas, to pick cotton for fifty cents a hundred. Got a few dollars, had an old Model T truck. Then we went to Gallup, New Mexico, to find cotton but it wasn't there, or else it wasn't ready yet. Then we went to Coolidge, Arizona, living all the time on 'Hoover Hogs' [jack rabbits] and black-eyed peas, maybe some pork for side meat. We made twenty-five miles an hour, maybe a hundred miles a day going down Route 66, and every other road too, looking for work. We went back to Oklahoma–every good Okie left more than once–and tried again and failed again. Did that more than once until finally we left for good, right down 66, splitting it wide open for six or seven days to Arizona. The wind was blowing, it was dry, the cotton wouldn't come up, everything went wrong. In the fall of '33 I went into the CCC camp, worked in the Grand Canyon on the Kaibab Trail. My dad was in a vet CCC camp. We made a buck a day and our board. It was some working for a dollar a day, but we were working and that was something.

"But the roughest of all the tough times was in Shafter, California, in the potato fields, boys. My God, how they worked you! Men were falling over like flies and two hundred other men were lined up at the fence waiting to take the fallen man's place when he dropped. But don't say it was all bad, boys, because it wasn't. Some of the finest evenings a man ever spent were in those cotton camps outside Coolidge. Under those mesquite trees, beside the tents, the Okies here, the Mexicans–everyone getting along. And the music of Mexico in the starlight. The strum of the guitars in those camps. It was beautiful." Today Okie Paul operates a country-music tavern–one of those places Glen Campbell calls "fightin' and dancin' clubs"–in North Sacramento. He also is the voice behind innumerable radio commercials in central California which always end: "Tell 'em Okie Paul sent ya." His tavern is called Detour Inn after the song he lived as well as composed: "Detour, There's a Muddy Road Ahead."

Like Mrs. Scott and other Okies we talked to, Okie Paul is proud of his survival and rich in his experience. He also senses the spiritual connection he has with the earliest pioneers who traveled the 35th parallel route West. As a parting word, he told us: "I'm one jump ahead of you fellows. I've been there, I know I can do it. You boys don't know if you can. And you know, the truth is it wasn't so bad, boys, it wasn't so bad. Think of those fellows who came first, crossed that desert, ate lizards, fought the Indians. Think of that, boys, think of that. Those boys had it hard. I used to think of them and that was hard times."

At the end of Route 66, at the end of our ride back into the history of the great migrant route, Okie Paul remembered Marcy, Simpson, and Beale. He didn't know their names, he didn't know the years of their trip or the purpose of those who came after, but he knew about the road, knew that, like him, they had traveled it and survived. Like all of the Okies we interviewed who followed Route 66 during the Depression, Okie Paul seems to epitomize what California writer Gerald Haslam *(Okies: Selected Stories)* describes as that quality that is "tough, able, complex." "Perfection," Haslam says, "is not an Okie characteristic, but a blues-like ability to accept adversity with grace and grit is. And they have not forgotten how to laugh at themselves."

Nor have they forgotten the travails of forty years ago, these keen historians; and their memories are the final heritage of the road. Today, in place of the old color and life are the familiar plastic and glass and concrete rest stops and off-ramp clusters of service stations and motels and quick-food restaurants. No more homemade apple pies, real milk shakes, real coffee; no more place to skinny-dip in the Colorado on a hot afternoon, farms with fruit stands run by the youngest kid in the family, advertisements reading "Chew Mail Pouch" on the sides of barns; no more Burma Shave rhymes, Giant Snake farms, Teepee motels, and "rooms for rent." Route 66, the Osage Trail, the Wire Road, the mail route, the emigrant road, the Main Street of America, has vanished almost without a trace. The mother road is a ghost road.

Thomas W. Pew, Jr., a free-lance writer living in Tucson, Arizona, has contributed regularly to such publications as Smithsonian Magazine, The Nation, The Progressive, *and* Defenders of Wildlife.

CAFE
OPEN
DRINK
NEHI
ICE COLD
REASONABLE
DINNERS &
SANDWICHES
10 2 4
Dr Pepper
CAFE

The sunlight began to dim hours before sunset and the clean, fresh air acquired a peculiar density as a giant, black dust cloud approached from the northwest. More than a thousand feet high, the cloud swept southeast and extended in a straight line as far as the eye could see, rolling and tumbling like a great wall of muddy water. Hundreds of birds flew in panic before it. People who saw the dust storm coming fled quickly to their homes to tape windows, jam rugs under doors, cover furniture, and hang wet sheets across rooms. Wet towels were held over mouths and noses as the premature but total darkness descended. Homes rattled with the force of the storm, and as the dust sifted in and piled up beneath keyholes, breathing became labored and gave way to choking. Spring, 1935, had come to the southern Great Plains.

The people of this region were entering their fourth year of dust storms, and the traditional "blow months" of February, March, and April. The wind erosion hazard was the greatest in a 97-million-acre section, which an Associated Press reporter writing for the Washington, D.C., *Evening Star* casually but appropriately termed the "Dust Bowl." The Soil Conservation Service adopted the term almost immediately and used it when referring to the wind-blown, drought-stricken area encompassing eastern Colorado and New Mexico, western Kansas, and the panhandles of Texas and Oklahoma.

The dust storms of the thirties were not new to the southern plains, but in that decade their frequency and severity reached an all-time high largely because of the seven-year drought that began during the summer of 1931 following the great plow-up of the teens and twenties. High prices during World War I had stimulated plains farmers to break new lands, and rainfall was sufficient enough to allow, if not encourage, this expansion. When the wheat prices collapsed in the early 1920's, plainsmen used the newly adopted one-way disc plow to break more sod and plant more wheat to offset the economic loss. Between 1909 and 1929 Great Plains farmers broke thirty-two million acres of sod. Much of the expansion occurred in the southern Great Plains, where wheat acreage increased 200 per cent between 1925 and 1931, and in many counties it ranged from 400 to 1000 per cent.

As the farmers worked this newly broken land, most gave little thought to plowing under crop residues to increase soil humus, either burning them off or leaving them to be eaten by livestock until every bit of vegetation was consumed, exposing the soil to the wind.

Ordinarily, the southern plains receives approximately eighteen inches of annual precipitation. This amount is adequate for a satisfactory crop yield only when it is carefully conserved, but farmers seldom tried to preserve moisture in the subsoil. Furthermore, snows were insufficient to protect the soil, and winter contributed to erosion by loosening the ground with alternate freezing and thawing. The drought of 1931 began a chain reaction: crop failure followed by the abandonment of lands, followed by relentless wind erosion, followed by dust storms, followed by further crop failure.

By spring, 1934, wind erosion in the Dust Bowl was so serious that most farmers and ranchers were willing to adopt the appropriate measures to bring their soil under control. The Soil Conservation Service, created in 1935, used private lands to demonstrate proper soil-conserving techniques and aided farmers in beginning a massive soil conservation program that stressed emergency tillage to trap blowing soil, contour-plowing and terracing to retain moisture, strip-cropping to provide a soil-holding root system, regrassing blowing lands, and grazing management.

In order to halt dust storms completely,

DUST!

by R. Douglas Hurt

grazing lands had to be restored. Although approximately sixty-five million acres in the Dust Bowl remained in grass through the 1930's, the carrying capacity of these grasslands was far below normal. Overgrazing and drought had decreased the height and density of the grass to the extent that the soil was completely denuded in some areas. By December, 1934, for example, nearly all the native grass cover near Las Animas, Colorado, was smothered in drifting soil, and by spring, 1935, the pasture lands in western Kansas were 35 per cent below normal in growth. Similar lands were drifting badly in Texas and Oklahoma. With the guidance of the Soil Conservation Service, ranchers began to practice pasture-resting by rotating their grazing herds. They also began to contour-furrow their pastures to decrease runoff and hold as much precipitation as possible.

Despite the efforts of Dust Bowl farmers and ranchers to bring their lands under control, the dust storms increased each year from 1934 to 1938 in the southern plains. But during the summer of 1938 good rains fell over most of the area, enabling farmers to plant soil-holding crops on much of the blowing land, and by spring, 1939, the Dust Bowl had shrunk to the smallest area since 1932. Ample rainfall also came in the summer and autumn of 1940, and for the remainder of the decade the plains received above-average precipitation.

During the ten-year period from 1941 through 1950 most Dust Bowl farmers and ranchers prospered. Bumper crops were the rule, and prices were high. Land that could not be sold for $3 to $4 per acre in the 1930's now brought $40 to $60 per acre. During this time another big plow-up occurred in the southern Great Plains. Farmers broke about four million acres. High prices for meat also encouraged heavy stocking of pasture lands.

Rainfall was below normal in many sections of the southern plains during 1950. By 1952 severe drought had returned to the region, and with the drought came the dust. Blowing soil was particularly bad on the newly plowed lands, on the poorer wheat lands, and on the overgrazed pasture lands. Serious dust storms in the spring of 1954 and 1955 once again darkened the sky and sometimes reduced visibility to zero, drifted soil along fence rows, created sand dunes in some fields, and ruined crops.

Although wind erosion affected a larger area than it had twenty years earlier, the region did not revert to the severe conditions of the 1930's—principally because of the conservation techniques practiced during the previous two decades. As a result, some of the worst blow areas of the 1930's were not critically affected by the drought and wind of the 1950's. Furthermore, Dust Bowl farmers were better prepared financially to handle the drought and blowing soil, and the federal government once again provided funds for emergency tillage.

Today, the southern Great Plains is experiencing another drought. The deficiency in rainfall has stunted vegetation growth, and the wind is blowing the soil. But this is not to say that the "black blizzards," a characteristic of the 1930's, will necessarily return. Dust Bowl farmers, as a whole, now know how to handle blowing soil and, more importantly, recognize the need to keep protective cover crops on the soil to prevent a serious wind erosion problem. But they may have to make other major adjustments in their current practices; they must realize the value of planting more drought-resistant crops and of reducing grazing on pasture lands.

Another Dust Bowl is not inevitable. But it is possible.

R. Douglas Hurt is a Smithsonian Fellow in the History of Science and Technology.

LIBRARY OF CONGRESS

ARUCH En CHERIDYN BARBAROSSA
Koningen van Algiers.

The U.S. vs. International Terrorists

by Gaddis Smith

A Chapter From Our Past

Opposite: the Barbarossa brothers, who ruled Algiers in the sixteenth century and established piracy as a form of diplomacy
NEW YORK PUBLIC LIBRARY, RARE BOOK DIVISION

Terrorists hijack an airplane and hold the passengers for ransom. A merchant ship is seized by the forces of a small, disorganized state. The United States retaliates. The ship and crew are rescued, but many lives are lost.

Such events are shocking yet familiar manifestations of the apparent lawlessness of the modern world. But if we could bring back an American of the late eighteenth and early nineteenth centuries and ask his comment, he would show little surprise except, perhaps, at the changes in the technology of transportation. He would have seen the United States confront a similar phenomenon: the Barbary pirates.

There were in the eighteenth century four Barbary states lining the north coast of Africa from Egypt westward to the Atlantic. Morocco on the Atlantic was an independent state ruled by an emperor. Algiers, Tunis, and Tripoli—corresponding roughly to the modern states of Algeria, Tunisia, and Libya—were nominally part of the Ottoman (Turkish) Empire, but were in fact brazenly independent of Constantinople. The rulers of all four states maintained their revenue and power by preying on commerce—capturing ships and cargoes, making and ransoming slaves. Nations desiring immunity from these depredations could get it for a heavy price: continual tribute in cash and gifts and large sums to negotiate and renew so-called peace treaties.

The enslaved captives were usually treated according to the amount of ransom each would bring. Captains and distinguished passengers were well fed and housed. Some became advisers to their captors; others were allowed to open taverns or otherwise go into business; all were allowed to correspond with friends and representatives of their own governments in order to raise the money for ransom. Common sailors, illiterate and friendless, men of uncertain nationality and without influence, were put to hard labor building breakwaters and other public works. Their food was terrible and they were clothed in rags. With scant medical attention many of them died. Since they were worth relatively little in ransom, the Barbary rulers valued them for their labor as slaves.

The naval power of the Barbary states was enough to terrorize lightly armed or unarmed merchant ships, but was insignificant compared to that of any major European navy. Why then was the piracy condoned, even encouraged by the payment of tribute? The answer is that large, wealthy maritime powers such as Great Britain found it expedient to pay the price of protection for British commerce in order to keep the pirates in existence as a threat to smaller commercial rivals such as Sweden, the Netherlands, Naples, and—after 1783—the United States. London merchants believed, Benjamin Franklin observed, "that if there were no Algiers, it would be worth England's while to build one."

Had the smaller powers banded together in a naval alliance, they could have put an end to piracy. They talked of coalition, but did not act effectively. The result was that the Barbary states maintained a constant state of war with one or more of the smaller European nations. Algiers, for example, might make peace if the price was right and sell a batch of captives back to freedom. A few years later, with the supply of slaves depleted, Algiers would find some pretext, some alleged insult or failure to pay tribute on time, and casually declare war again. The captain of a merchant vessel from a small country could never know when he began a voyage whether by the time he reached the North African coast his country would be at war with one or more of the Barbary states.

Before the war for independence Americans traded safely in the Mediterranean under the protection purchased for all British subjects by the government in London. American peace negotiators in Paris in 1782 tried to persuade the British to continue this service for independent Yankee shipping. No luck. A few British statesmen had fraternal feelings toward the United States, but the majority agreed with the influential publicist Lord Sheffield that the upstart Americans should be punished by the most severe economic policy that Parliament could devise. Sheffield wrote in 1783 that the United States would not "have a very free trade in the Mediterranean; it

CULVER

John Adams (above) and Thomas Jefferson were equally outraged.

NEW-YORK HISTORICAL SOCIETY

will not be the interest of any of the great maritime powers to protect them there from the Barbary States. . . . The Americans cannot protect themselves from the latter; they cannot pretend to a navy." American diplomats asked France to guard the new nation's Mediterranean trade. The French promised only to provide their "good offices" when the United States dealt with the Barbary states. The cost to France and the benefit to the United States of good offices were the same: zero. Vergennes, the French foreign minister, was quite willing to give advice to the Americans, but it all boiled down to a polite reiteration of the comment that the United States did indeed have a serious problem.

Thus, Americans were on their own. Congress in 1784 instructed Benjamin Franklin, John Adams, and Thomas Jefferson to negotiate treaties with the Barbary states. Franklin soon returned from Paris to the United States, his place as minister to France taken by Jefferson, and John Adams assumed the post of minister to Great Britain. From Paris and London the two men grappled with the question of the Barbary states and directed some lesser diplomats in attempted negotiations.

At first the problem was theoretical. There were no American ships seized in 1783 or 1784 because few American shipowners had yet returned to trading after the devastation of war. But soon vessels began to resume the important prewar trade with Spain, Portugal, and the Mediterranean. Before 1776 an estimated one hundred American colonial vessels a year had carried fish, grain, flour, and rum to southern Europe. Americans confidently expected that the volume of trade and profit would double in the 1780's—but these high expectations were soon violently dashed.

On July 25, 1785, the schooner *Maria*, of Boston, Captain Isaac Stephens, was sailing toward the Strait of Gibralter and Cadiz, Spain. The sails of a vessel appeared on the horizon and came rapidly closer. She carried fourteen guns, flew the flag of Algiers, and quickly declared the *Maria* captive. Six days later the ship *Dauphin*, of Boston, Captain Richard O'Brien, met the same fate. The twenty-one officers and men of the two vessels were carried to Algiers and slavery. They would be freed, the captors said, when the United States paid a heavy ransom and purchased a peace treaty. Did not the Americans understand that Algiers considered herself at war with all nations that had not agreed to pay regular tribute? The news of these warlike, or piratical, seizures soon reached Jefferson and Adams. As Woodrow Wilson was to say about German submarine attacks in 1917, the United States now faced "overt acts."

For a moment Jefferson and Adams saw some hope. An agent sent to Morocco came back with a quick and misleadingly easy treaty that cost only $20,000 and, while it lasted, protected American shipping from Moroccan capture.

But the American agent sent to Algiers reported that the twenty-one captives would be freed upon payment of $59,496. Captains were $6,000 per head, mates and passengers $4,000, sailors $1,400. Eleven per cent was to be added "according to custom." Jefferson, Adams, and John Jay, the Secretary to Congress for Foreign Affairs, then began a searching discussion of the connection of foreign and domestic policy, the use of violence to achieve objectives, and the difficulty of defining and acting upon the national interest. The issues raised and the arguments used so early in our national history have echoed down to the present.

What should a nation do when its merchant shipping is seized and its citizens are held captive by a small, distant enemy whose only objective is to collect ransom and perpetual bribes as the price of refraining from further captures? Swallow pride and pay? Abandon trade in dangerous waters? Seek assistance from other nations? Or incur the expense of a fighting navy in order to free the captives and punish, perhaps even destroy, the captors? The questions become more difficult to answer when the offended nation is without a reliable federal revenue, without a navy, even without an executive branch to carry through a policy. This was the case for the United States government under the Articles of Confederation in 1786.

Jefferson approached the problem by asking what kind of people Americans ought to be. "Were I to indulge my own theory, I should wish them to practise neither commerce nor navigation, but to stand with respect to Europe, precisely on the footing of China. We should thus avoid wars. . . ." But Jefferson admitted that, despite his own predilection, the American people would turn to the sea. They believe "it is necessary for us to take a share in the occupation of the ocean." An equal share of the ocean would lead to wars and threats of war. A navy was a first necessity. "Weakness provokes insult and injury, while a condition to punish, often prevents them."

Confronted with the spectacle of Americans chained to slavery and hard labor in Algiers, Jefferson became uncharacteristically impetuous and emotional. The pirates were an unspeakable affront. He gagged at the prospect of rewarding criminality through bribery. He was hot for an American navy, hot for punishing the "Algerines," hot for victory at the cannon's mouth. He gathered naval intelligence with relish and diligence, delighted in proposing tactics and strategy, scorned the fighting abilities of the Barbary mariners, and dreamed of setting John Paul Jones loose among them. On this question Jefferson was not the cautious figure familiar to students of his Presidency, but rather a vicarious commodore pacing the quarterdeck of his mind, sending ships to battle and disposing his forces.

John Adams in London played the cool skeptic. Adams agreed that "Avarice and Fear are the only Agents at Algiers," but he doubted that Congress had the will to raise a force sufficient to use fear as an instrument. Furthermore, he calculated that war would be ten times more expensive than tribute "and when you leave off fighting you must pay as much money as it would cost you now for peace." To do nothing would mean abandoning a trade worth "more than half a million sterling a year."

The problem, said Adams to Jefferson, was Congress. Until Congress imposed regular taxes and raised a sufficient revenue "you and I as well as every other Servant of the United States in Europe ought to go home, give up all Points, and let all our Exports and Imports be done in European Bottoms. My Indignation is roused beyond all Patience to see the People . . . in a Torpor, and see them a Prey to every Robber, Pirate and Cheat in Europe." Adams, the cantankerous New Englander, exaggerated regional differences over foreign policy in the United States and put the blame for impotence on the Southern states. He said he was as ready in theory to fight as Jefferson. If his Virginia friend could persuade the South, Adams promised that the other states "from Pennsylvania northward would not object. It would be a good occasion to begin a Navy."

Jefferson disagreed with Adams' arithmetic and did not share his pessimism. In a famous letter on July 11, 1786, he marshaled all his arguments in favor of war. "1. Justice is in favor of this opinion. 2. Honor favors it. 3. It will procure us respect in Europe, and respect is a safe-guard to interest. 4. It will arm the federal head with the safest of all instruments of coercion over their delinquent members and prevent them from using what would be less safe. . . . 5. I think it least expensive. 6. Equally effectual."

The fourth point was the most interesting, for it raised the issue of the domestic political uses of a foreign policy based on armed force. Jefferson at this stage, a year before the Constitutional Convention, was an unabashed Federalist. He saw the possibility of disunion and the need for power to prevent it. But he feared a standing *army* as a dangerous instrument of coercion. A navy could bring pressure on coastal cities, could coerce by controlling trade; but it could not strike inland, could not attack the hearth of Jefferson's beloved husbandman.

Jefferson and Adams agreed that the United States would get no assistance from France and Great Britain. They even suspected that the British were encouraging the Barbary states to attack American shipping. But, said Jefferson, the United States might be able to negotiate a naval alliance with some of the lesser maritime states. He wrote to his friend James Monroe at home that if the United States could supply "a couple of frigates, a convention might be formed with those powers establishing a perpetual cruise," which would bring the pirates to reason. With or without such a confederacy, the United States must have a naval force. "It will be said, there is no money in the treasury. There never will be money in the treasury, till the Confederacy shows its teeth."

While Jefferson waxed ever more enthusiastic and made calculations of how many naval guns would be necessary and how much each gun would cost, Adams grew more resigned to national failure. He said that Jefferson's estimates of naval requirements were far too low. No war should be started unless the nation had the means and determination to fight to a finish, which meant "finally breaking up these nests of Banditti." But, alas, the "States are so backward that they will do nothing for some years."

The man in the best position to judge what the states would do was John Jay, Secretary to Congress for Foreign Affairs, closest equivalent to Secretary of State in a government without an executive branch. Jay was an intelligent but somewhat arrogant aristocrat who looked on the Congress he served with contempt. Never in the twentieth century did any believer in presidential power heap as much scorn on the legislature for supposed lack of vision or courage in foreign affairs.

When Jay first learned that Algiers had declared war on the United States, he had some hope. "If we act properly," he wrote Adams, "I shall not be very sorry for it. In my opinion it may lay the foundation for a navy, and tend to draw us more closely into a federal system." And to the Congress he said: "This war does not strike me as a great evil. The more we are ill-treated abroad the more we shall unite and consolidate at home.

John Jay (above) to Jefferson: "I should prefer War to Tribute."

NATIONAL PORTRAIT GALLERY, SMITHSONIAN INSTITUTION

NEW-YORK HISTORICAL SOCIETY

BETTMANN ARCHIVE

Besides, as it may become a nursery for seamen, and lay the foundation for a respectable navy, it may eventually prove more beneficial than otherwise." And to Jefferson he declared: "If our Government could draw forth the Resources of the Country which . . . are abundant, I should prefer War to Tribute, and carry on our Mediterranean Trade in Vessels armed and manned at the Public Expence."

Congress, however, was in no mood to tax and spend; nor could it compel contributions from the states. An infinitesimal sum—$80,000—was available for negotiations. Adams and Jefferson discovered from an ambassador of Tripoli in London that the annual amounts demanded by Tripoli and Tunis were far in excess of "the Limits of Congress, and of Reason." Furthermore, peace with Tripoli and Tunis was of no value as long as there was no peace with Algiers, since Algiers could block the entrance of American shipping into the Mediterranean. Nothing was done.

Jay's optimism evaporated quickly and by 1787, with the Constitutional Convention about to convene, he had ceased to make any significant effort to persuade Congress to act. He took masochistic delight in America's troubles on the theory that only complete degradation could compel the people to improve their condition by forming a powerful government. In an address to the people of New York in 1788, he lamented: "Our shipyards have almost ceased to disturb the repose of the neighbourhood by the noise of the axe and the hammer; and while foreign flags fly triumphantly above our highest houses, the American stars seldom do more than shed a few feeble rays about the humbler masts of river sloops and coasting schooners. . . . The Algerines exclude us from the Mediterranean and adjacent countries; and we are neither able to purchase nor to command the free use of those seas."

By then the old government under the Articles of Confederation was fading away, unlamented by Jay and those who shared his vision. The new Constitution was before the states for ratification. In 1789 the Constitution came into force with George Washington as President and John Adams, home from London, as Vice President. Soon Jefferson would return from Paris to become the nation's first Secretary of State.

The Constitution did not bring about a magical, instantaneous change. In Algiers the despondent American captives from the *Maria* and the *Dauphin* were still enslaved, except for seven dead of the plague. Year by year the asking price for ransom had gone up, and an effort by Jefferson to employ a religious order called the Mathurins, dedicated to ransoming captives, had come to nought. American trade to the Mediterranean was at a complete halt.

The situation was static for more than a year under the new government, while Congress and the executive were busy establishing procedures and getting organized. But late in 1790 Secretary of State Jefferson received a detailed proposal from a European friend (whose identity is a mystery to this day) for carrying war to the Mediterranean, for seizing rich booty, taking Barbary prisoners, even selling them into slavery. Jefferson was delighted. He wrote two reports to Congress and the President on the state of Mediterranean trade and on the captives in Algiers, recommending war.

Congress discussed the reports in closed session. The best record of what was said is the journal of Senator William Maclay of Pennsylvania. Sometimes called "the first Jeffersonian," Maclay reacted with deep suspicion. Jefferson's reports, he said, "seemed to breathe resentment, and abounded with martial estimates in a naval way. We have now fourteen unhappy men in captivity in Algiers. I wish we had them relieved, and the trade to the Mediterranean abandoned. There can be no chance of our wanting a market for our produce."

The Senate responded in January, 1791, with the oft-quoted resolution "That the trade of the United States to the Mediterranean cannot be protected but by a naval force, and that it will be proper to resort to the same as soon as the state of the public finances will admit." Maclay, a classic agrarian antimilitarist, opposed the resolution. He deplored the fact that the taxes that would support a navy were called "bonds of our Union" by some of his fellow senators. "War is often entered into to answer domestic, not foreign purposes. I fear such was the design of the present report. It was even talked how many ships should be fitted out and of what force." Maclay believed that Barbary affairs were a pretext of "the court" to build a powerful central government in order to annihilate state government. An army for unnecessary war with the Indians and a navy would require "a host of revenue officers." The result would be "farewell freedom in America."

In 1793 the situation for American trade grew worse. For several years Portugal had been at war with Algiers. Now a Portuguese-Algerian truce enabled the corsairs of Algiers to sally again past the Strait of Gibraltar into the Atlantic. In October and November, 1793, eleven American vessels were captured. Over one hundred more officers and men became prisoners. This time the captors disregarded the distinction

BOTH: BETTMANN ARCHIVE

The depredations of the Barbary pirates moved nineteenth-century artists to romantic images—fierce shipboard encounters, and captives at hard labor (opposite page); capture of an American schooner (left); and (above) European women carried off by corsairs to a fate that could only be whispered.

James Madison urged war, and got it.
COLONIAL WILLIAMSBURG

between officers and men. Moses Morse, master of the brig *Jane*, wrote that "we were all of us Strip't of evry thing, even part of our old sea cloths on our backs were taken, and the day after our arrival here was put in Iron's, & a chain of about 30 lb. and in that situation . . . was put to the Hardest Labour, and continue at the same every day. they have since taken off our Iron's, but the cruel treatment is too much for me to discribe." Another captain wrote that "Death would be a great relief & more welcome than a continuance of our present situation."

At last Congress moved. The law creating the navy and authorizing the construction of six ships was passed March 27, 1794. But still Jefferson's preferred policy against the Barbary states was delayed. The wars of the French Revolution soon embroiled the United States in potential conflict with Great Britain or France. The pirates would have to wait to receive their medicine. Congress authorized ransom and tribute instead of war, and in 1795 peace was made with Algiers upon the promise to pay $642,500 plus an annual tribute in the form of naval stores. The surviving prisoners were freed.

By 1797 the United States had spent almost a million dollars to keep the peace. Nearly a third of this was in naval stores and weaponry, including a superb frigate. Here was the first time the United States provided a form of foreign military aid. The Dey of Algiers was so pleased with the quality of American warships that, with the approval of President John Adams and the Congress, he purchased several more. As one historian has commented, it seemed as if the United States was about to become "the arsenal of piracy."

Meanwhile the new American Navy was in combat for the first time—against France in the undeclared war of 1798–99. In 1800 the quarrel with France was papered over and Jefferson was elected President. He inherited a lean, combat-tested navy and a Barbary policy of tribute that he had earlier deplored. In 1786 he had warned that a purchased peace would not last. He was right. In 1800 the Barbary states wanted more tribute and presents.

President Jefferson despatched a fighting squadron to the Mediterranean. It arrived in the summer of 1801 just after Tripoli declared war on the United States. Fighting began—desultory at first but mounting in intensity as American naval strength increased and Commodore Edward Preble assumed command. A score of naval heroes were made and enough tales of high adventure were written to enthrall schoolboys for ten generations. The most significant event was the loss to Tripoli of the frigate *Philadelphia*, Captain William Bainbridge, after the ship ran on a reef while pursuing a Tripolitanian cruiser. Bainbridge and his crew of 307 were captured, swelling the ranks of Barbary captives. The enlisted men were put to hard labor. Subsequently, Lieutenant Stephen Decatur became a hero for destroying the *Philadelphia* in a daring raid. The details of combat, however, are less significant than the policy considerations.

Jefferson in 1786 had underestimated the naval force required to subdue Algiers and he made the same mistake during the war with Tripoli. As Secretary of State in 1791 he came under attack from antimilitarists for proposing to use any force at all; as President he was criticized for failing to use enough force. One of his sharpest critics was Federalist Senator William Plumer of New Hampshire, who thought it "*bad policy, & base wickedness* for a president to send brave men where they must inevitable [*sic*] be destroyed for the want of an adequate force. Had he sent a sufficient number of men & ships it would have been expensive—it might have endangered his reputation for economy & lessened his popularity with the rabble but would most probably have saved the lives of deserving men. He ought to have sent something more than a sufficiency—enough to inspire the Men with confidence—to guard against accidents—& to insure success."

Another who shared Plumer's reservations was William Eaton, an adventurer with a dubious past, an active imagination, and a taste for military glory. Eaton's solution was for the United States to provide combat support on land for one Hamet Caramanli, a Tripolitanian seeking to overthrow his brother and regain the throne. Caramanli, in gratitude, would then make peace with the United States and maintain a friendly posture. He would be our man in Tripoli. It was an early example of the policy of controlling another country's behavior by trying to overthrow its government.

Eaton failed to gain Jefferson's full support, but, undeterred, returned to the Mediterranean, raised a ragtag army, and led a remarkable desert campaign on behalf of Caramanli. Just as Eaton thought he was on the verge of victory, Tobias Lear, American consul general in Algiers, came to Tripoli and paid $60,000 ransom for some American captives and signed a peace treaty. Caramanli was left dangling, a pitiful suppliant for charity from the United States. Eaton and his friends excoriated Jefferson and Lear, but the Senate in 1805 ratified the peace Lear had made.

The year 1805 also brought the first Moslem envoy to the United States. Sidi Soliman

William Bainbridge (top) was humiliatingly captured, but later returned to fight again; William Eaton (above) raised a motley desert army to attack the Tripolitans from the rear.

TOP: NEW YORK PUBLIC LIBRARY, PICTURE COLLECTION. ABOVE: HENRY E. HUNTINGTON LIBRARY AND ART GALLERY, SAN MARINO, CALIF.

Mellimelni arrived from Tunis with a large and colorful retinue. In Washington he was a major tourist attraction but was ineffectual in negotiating a dispute arising out of the American blockade of Tripoli during which some Tunisian vessels were seized. Mellimelni toured several American cities before returning to Tunis, where, in 1807, Tobias Lear found the Tunisians amenable to a settlement—perhaps because of reports by Mellimelni on the size and power of the United States.

During the next decade the Barbary question nearly disappeared from the agenda of American foreign policy, overshadowed by the controversies with Great Britain that culminated in the war of 1812. American naval forces returned to home waters and fought valiantly in that war. Nearly all American merchant vessels also withdrew from the Mediterranean. But in 1812 Algiers broke her treaty with the United States, captured an American vessel, and enslaved the crew. Soon after peace with Great Britain was signed on Christmas Eve, 1814, President James Madison opened the last chapter of the Barbary story by asking Congress to declare war on Algiers. Congress complied.

Two powerful squadrons—one under Stephen Decatur and the other under William Bainbridge—sailed to the Mediterranean and inflicted heavy damage on the Algerians. The Dey of Algiers signed, almost literally at the cannon's mouth, a treaty abolishing tribute in every form. He then procrastinated about putting the treaty into effect. The United States threatened more force. At the same time the British and the Dutch abandoned the old policy of tribute and administered a ferocious bombardment against the fortifications and fleet of Algiers. The Dey capitulated. Tunis and Tripoli, intimidated by the display of power, also turned gentle. Barbary piracy, as an act of governments, was over. The residual piracy of isolated private bands was easily suppressed. Henceforth, until the world wars of the twentieth century, American shipping traversed the Mediterranean in safety.

Some reflections are in order. The final destruction of Barbary piracy was attributed by most Americans to their own determination and naval prowess. The importance of Great Britain's decision no longer to play the tribute game was overlooked, while patriotic naval heroes—Preble, Decatur, Bainbridge—filled the stage. The affair lost all complexity and emerged as melodrama in the popular mind. The debates within the American government over the use of force, the price of honor, and the sometimes hidden connections between domestic and foreign policy were overlooked. Yet these debates contain more drama and lasting interest than a score of naval engagements and expeditions "to the shores of Tripoli."

The simplified version of the Barbary wars contributed its bit to the myth of American righteousness and omnipotence. Subconsciously, later Americans may have equated all foes from "backward" countries with the Barbary pirates: contemptible bandits motivated by fear and avarice alone. Withdrawal from the Mediterranean, tribute, or war may have been the only alternatives in dealing with the Barbary states at the turn of the eighteenth century. But those states were throwbacks to the middle ages rather than forerunners of the modern "Third World."

Thus the Barbary experience should not be pressed too closely to provide lessons for the present. It is as important to know the differences as it is to note the similarities between Barbary pirates and modern hijackers. The Barbary predators were not motivated by ideological passion. They led no fervent national movement. They were, for all their violence and threats, entrepreneurs playing the game of snatching and selling men. They calculated profit against loss, declared war, made peace, and haggled over prices with equal nonchalance. When faced with superior force they backed off and ultimately, when the major powers no longer found it convenient to tolerate piracy, withdrew altogether from the game. The roots of modern terrorism are far deeper, far more entwined with powerful grievances and ideological objectives. The surface similarity with the Barbary piracy is there, but the solutions today are infinitely more difficult.

Gaddis Smith is a Professor of History at Yale University where he teaches both diplomatic and maritime history.

by Nat Brandt

He was a study in contrasts: an inventive genius who discovered the alternating-current system that lit up the world, but an inept businessman who died in poverty; an extrovert showman who dazzled audiences by lighting without wires a bulb held in his hand, but a reclusive bachelor whose greatest love, he once confided, was a sickly pigeon he had nursed back to health. He was a pacifist, but dabbled with "death rays," a writer of poems though he kept no written records of his experiments, a visionary who foresaw interstellar communication but disparaged Einstein's theories.

His name was Nikola Tesla, and it is surprising, in view of his great contributions to mankind, that he still remains in the shadow of Thomas Edison.

The two men knew—and disliked—each other. Their enmity focused on disagreement over the merits of direct versus alternating current. In the end Tesla triumphed, but it was a victory without laurels. When he was informed that he would share with Edison the Nobel Prize for physics in 1912, he refused to accept the honor. He was, he said, a discoverer of new principles, while Edison was only an inventor of useful appliances. As a result, neither man received the award, but today Edison's name is almost synonymous with electricity, while Tesla's is perpetuated only as that of a type of a transformer coil.

Raised in a rural Croatian village of modern-day Yugoslavia where he was born in 1856, Tesla, while still a child, was fascinated one day to see a snowball roll down a mountainside, growing in size and speed until it brought on an avalanche. The incident impressed him with the tremendous forces locked up in nature, and he later fashioned toys that harnessed the power of water and even the wing beats of insects. He also showed an uncanny ability to visualize models, drawings, and experiments without writing them out.

While studying electrical engineering in Austria in 1878, Tesla first turned his attention to the problems of generating direct current (which flows in only one direction). Four years later, a solution came to him in typical fashion. He was walking in a park in Budapest, reciting a poem to a companion, when he suddenly stopped, became rigid as if in a trance, and said, "Watch me!" Picking up a twig, he drew in the dirt a complete diagram of a rotating magnetic field. It was the key to unlocking the secret of alternating current (which reverses direction in a circuit at regular intervals) and led to his invention of the rotary motor, the polyphase power system, generators, dynamos, and transformers—all in use today.

An unhappy stint with a company in Paris that used Edison's direct-current patents prompted Tesla to leave for America, where he hoped to find more willing ears for his ideas. In 1884 he arrived in New York with four cents in his pocket, some poems and technical articles he had written, plans for a flying machine, and a letter of introduction to Edison, who hired him to work in his plant.

Tesla tried to persuade Edison to abandon the d.c. system because it provided only weak illumination and necessitated a power station every few blocks. Edison was not only unconvinced but also attacked Tesla's a.c. system as dangerous, if not lethal. In 1886, Tesla quit because he felt Edison had reneged on a promise to pay him $50,000 for developing dynamos.

He went to work as a day laborer, even dug ditches, until he could get backing for a company of his own. Tesla took out the first of some seven hundred patents and in 1888 delivered before the American Institute of Electrical Engineers what is now considered a classic lecture on his discoveries that brought him to the attention of George Westinghouse, an Edison rival.

With Westinghouse's backing, Tesla accepted the task of illuminating the 1893 Columbian Exposition in Chicago. The result was a spectacular success, as was Tesla's own stage performance in which one million volts of high-frequency alternating current passed through his body without harming him—an effective refutation of Edison's charges. Later, the Tesla-Westinghouse partnership converted the hydraulic power of Niagara Falls into electrical energy and transmitted it to Buffalo, twenty-two miles away. By 1903 all new generating stations, including Edison's, were employing Tesla's a.c. system, and he was a celebrity.

Tesla often talked about making millions, but he generously tore up his contract with Westinghouse to save Westinghouse from losing his company, would not sue patent infringers, and dismissed the idea of manufacturing his own equipment. "This is small-time stuff," he said. "I cannot be bothered with it."

He continued to attract financial backers, but two of his later experiments aroused skepticism. To prove the earth is a reservoir of energy, Tesla built a giant 4,000,000-volt oscillator in Colorado Springs, Colorado; it produced an eerie display of electrical fireworks and inadvertently knocked out the city's power supply. Then, in 1902, he erected a huge tower on Long Island, vowing to illuminate a fair in Europe with power transmitted across the ocean without wires. Before it was completed, however, he ran out of money.

His eccentricities, too, invited ridicule. He had odd eating habits and a phobia about germs, worked with the shades drawn except during lightning storms, and boasted that he slept only two hours a night—except for once a year, when he slept for five hours to build up a reserve of body energy.

Tesla's writings anticipated radio, remote control, radar, medical diathermy, fluorescent and neon lamps, but in such vague, almost mystical terms that fellow scientists came to ignore them. By the time of his death in 1943 at the age of eighty-six, he was virtually forgotten.

Seven years earlier, Yugoslavia had honored him by establishing an institute in his name in Belgrade. The highest tribute accorded him by his adopted country was, ironically, the Edison Medal, which the American Institute of Electrical Engineers awarded him in 1917. Tesla turned it down at first because it was named for his bitter foe, and when he did agree to the presentation he had to be coaxed to the ceremony from a park where he was feeding pigeons.

COLLECTION OF DON DWIGGINS

NIKOLA TESLA

The Adventures of a Haunted Whaling Man

The exacting, colorful, and often perilous career of a whaleman of the last century is known to most readers only through such fiction as *Moby Dick*. But many a real American went "down to the sea in ships" from East Coast whaling ports, experiencing the loneliness, exhilaration, and dangers that Herman Melville described. One of them was Robert Weir, a tormented nineteen-year-old, who in the summer of 1855 left his home in Cold Spring, New York, where he had worked in the local iron foundry. His father, Robert Walter Weir, was a noted painter who taught art at the military academy at West Point, across the Hudson River from Cold Spring.

Although without money, young Weir somehow made his way to the whaling seaport of New Bedford, Massachusetts, and there, using the name Wallace, he signed on board the bark *Clara Bell*. Unlike many of his contemporaries who ran away to sea simply for adventure, Weir was in debt and disgraced; his odyssey was a self-imposed punishment, prompted apparently by a gambling debt that had shamed his entire family.

On August 18, the *Clara Bell* left her berth and anchored in Buzzards Bay, waiting for a favorable tide to begin what would be a voyage of nearly three years across the South Atlantic, around South Africa's Cape of Good Hope, and into the Indian Ocean. During that time, Weir—a deeply religious young man—kept a journal, recording not only his anguished feelings of guilt and remorse, but the details of the voyage of the *Clara Bell*, the tedious and "sacriligeous" life aboard ship, the excitement of the whale hunt, and the exotic lands he visited. In the journal's margin he jotted drawings of ships, whales, and the scenes around him.

His remarkably introspective diary—from the collection of the G. W. Blunt White Library at Mystic Seaport Maritime Museum, and submitted to AMERICAN HERITAGE with introductory material by Professor Tamara K. Hareven of Harvard University—has never been published, though some of Weir's drawings have previously been reproduced. Accompanied by his illustrations, the following excerpts convey what life was like aboard a whaler more than 120 years ago. We begin as the *Clara Bell* prepares to set sail.

PRECEDING PAGE: *Charles S. Raleigh's eerie painting* Trying out at Night *shows a whaling bark on a moon-splashed ocean, its deck lit by the fire in the try works that rendered blubber into oil.*
NEW BEDFORD WHALING MUSEUM

1855 [August] 19th Sunday *Oh! if the folk at home knew what a field I am about to launch upon what would they say—What does dear father think—but I cannot turn back—I may just as well as not begin to cut my way in the world, now, rather than leave it till I am older. Spent this day sacriligeously in climbing about the rigging, didn't venture much—but guess I'll soon get used to it. Hurrah for hard times—at least I'd like to make myself feel so, but I scarcely dare look ahead—it seems rather dark. Have great anticipations of future independence. I shall* never never *call on father again—but I dare not speak his name. I have wronged him too much to be his son.*

20th Monday *A day to be remembered. The Captain came aboard a little after 9 o'clock, and we weighed anchor and set sail. Then came the first touch of work, in hauling up the anchor—such a pondrous thing is only fit to be buried at the bottom of the sea. I sincerely hope we shall not have the pleasure of dropping it till we again reach home—the chains were soon stowed between decks or rather in the chain pens—and the anchor's catted and lashed—and now we are on our way rejoicing. The first mate sent me aloft to slush the fore top gallant mast in the afternoon. The crew were divided into two watches, the Larboard and Starboard. I belong to the Mates or Larboard watch.*

21st Tuesday *Beginning to get seasick and disgusted. Land out of sight—feel awful. We have to work like horses and live like pigs—eyes beginning to open—rather dearly bought independence—however, get on the sunny side shortly I hope.*

22nd Wednesday *We are far very far out of sight of land—of sweet Ameriky. I was sent aloft on the lookout for whales and whatnots—And oh! how dreadfully sick I was. Saw two sharks, one about 12 ft. long and the other 5 or 6 ft. I felt very much tempted to throw myself to them for food. I can truly say I never was disgusted before in my life. . . . in the afternoon took my first trick at the helm—two weary, dreary, desolate hours—can a human being get toughened to all this—*

23rd Thursday *Sick as ever if not more so—but for all that have to work like a dog. . . . I must not forget to mention we were all called aft by the Captain before the Pilot left us—at the same time the 1st and 2nd mates picked their watches. Captain Robbins gave us a short harangue of which I noticed these few words—he'd give us plenty to eat and plenty to do—if we acted like men he'd treat us like men—no swearing etc. etc. etc. . . .* I turn in . . . *disgusted and thinking of home.*

24th Friday *Day commenced with a very stiff breeze, increased so much that we had to take in most of the sails; rained pretty hard in the evening—and I got wet and tired out tending the rigging and sails. Tumbled into my bunk with exhausted body and blistered hands—Romantic.*

25th Saturday *The wind still blows pretty hard and the decks are constantly washed by the waves—not quite recovered from sickness yet, but think I am getting better. I am absolutely sick and disgusted with the living and everything.*

26th Sunday *Commenced the day at the masthead feeling quite well; while looking about for whales or rather* nothing *(for I did not search the seas much as it was the Sabbath) I had pleasant thoughts of those I left so unkindly and abruptly but I console myself that it will be some relief to dear father, for me to be off his hands. I also amused myself by singing all the psalms and hymns, chants, etc., that dear Emma [his sister] and myself used to sing in our little Church—by that time my patience was pretty well exhausted and seasickness beginning to come on. My relief came very leisurely up the rigging—and now once more I find myself on deck, but am so sick from the rocking of the mast that I cannot read much in my bible as I intended, and can scarcely write. . . .*

27th Monday *Good breeze blowing—another week of toil before one—cheer up—we'll soon get used to hard work and look at it as play; but the feed—awful. The waters have not been quiet enough to allow writing with ease since we started. Often a big lurch of the ship will knock half the ideas out of ones head. I must give up now anyhow—*

My lookout at the masthead from 1 o'clock till 2. While there saw a school of cowfish and they appeared somewhat like the bodies of cows tumbling about in the water—saw plenty of flying fish—never imagined there were half so many in the sea—saw some land swallows one or two of which lit in the rigging—they did not remain long—rested an hour or more and then went home—*happy creatures. By 4 p.m. blowing quite a gale, plenty of rain—wind still increasing—both watches were sent aloft to take in sail—it must have been a rich sight to see us all scrambling up the shrouds, the ship was almost on her beam ends by the wind, and the spray dashing nearly to the fore-top. . . .*

30th Thursday *For 9 days we have been out of the sight of land—and for the last four days nothing has broken the line of the horizon—haven't heard the cry "there she blows" yet—but we are not left idle. Every day since we left home the hold has been overhauled or something otherwise done about the ship—. . .* innumerable *jobs. . . .*

31st Friday *Yesterday we had a half hours practice with the boats—I heard the call "man the boats" while at the mast head and down I had to scramble to be at my post for the Larboard boats. All four boats were lowered, and after maneuvering about for practice within a mile of the vessel—going through all the motions of harpooning and avoiding the struck whale, we raced to the ship and* our *boat beat. The crew of each boat amounts to six men—the mate, first, second or third, harpooner or boatsteerer, and 4 men. After the harpooner has fastened to a whale, he changes places with the mate, taking the steering oar while the mate goes in the bows of the boat and uses the lance to kill the leviathan. . . . So far the crew have deported themselves very peacefully—nearly half of them are Portuguese—don't like them—though I can make out to live peaceably. Our mate is a villain. I can see it but too plain . . . —the second mate is a boy—3rd mate a Gee* [*Portuguese*]. . . .

[***September***] ***2nd Sunday*** *Our Larboard watch commenced again at 3 o'clock this morning—the sea was in glorious commotion. We would see an enormous wave come rolling toward us—with every prospect of being overwhelmed—but no—God is there—our vessel would glide gently over it—through a brilliant dash of spray and foam. By 9 p.m. the moon broke through the clouds and showed the scene in all its grandeur. Oh—how wonderful art thou. Oh! most merciful Father in all thy works who can appreciate the beauties of Thy land. . . .*

17th Monday *Two short weeks have elapsed since I last got a chance to jot any items—it has been all work & no play—and I have not till now felt able to do anything in the writing line—. . . A great deal has happened during the first night above mentioned. We have laid off two ports—in the Azores—Flores & Fayal.*

At Flores we recruited ship—took on board any quantity of potatoes, pumpkins, onions, fowl, &c. Plenty of grapes—but to obtain them it is necessary to have plenty of money, but with tobacco we made pretty good trades—for apples, peaches, figs, and cheeses—donkey cheese at that—and right good & wholesome they were. I don't know that I ever enjoyed fruit and cheese so much—it seemed as though we had been deprived of them for years instead of a few weeks, it was long enough to make me long for something fresh—as I was so totally disgusted with shipfare—I am now getting more used to saltjunk, coffee & tea. I can't say what the coffee is made of, but it resembles that delicious beverage as much as ink resembles water—. . . As for the tea—if I only had some of the currant leaves off the bushes in our front yard, I'd feel grateful—but there is no use crying over spilt milk—get case hardened & go ahead—but I would like some one at home to have a sip of this same tea or coffee.

23rd Sunday *I am getting quite used to work now—and my hands can testify to that quite plainly—for they are as hard as horn inside—pulling & hauling on hard ropes—and the outside have a most beautiful . . . brown color—. . . .*

The manner in which the Sabbath is spent on board by nearly all—is truly deplorable, there is very little regard paid for the day—if we are not making & taking in sail all the while—and the weather is pleasant—most of the men will be seen squatting about the fore hatch smoking—dozing or growling—some read or wash—sew &c &c—but no thought is given to the welfare of the soul—And our noble 1st mate sets a most beautiful example by lounging on the quarter deck, the picture of idleness & misery—if he could he would like nothing better than to keep the crew hard at work Sundays as well as week days—

I shall indeed be thankful to get settled somewhere on land, where we can have a chance of improving the mind & choice of good companions. N'il desperandum.

September 24th Monday *Had a very pleasant day; in the afternoon lowered three boats for black-fish—a species of small whale—average length 20 ft. Our Larboard boat struck one and the waist boat fastened too—but both boats got loose. It seems quite natural to be rowing about. It is a sport I always liked—though I never rowed in such seas before—for, though it was a calm day—the waves were higher than I ever pulled over before—We chased the fish some four miles from the ship—and when we lost sight of them set sail with a good breeze for the ship—Our boat as usual was first & foremost—and we already pride ourselves on being a pretty smart crew, and a heavy one. I must not forget to mention about our scrubbing decks; every evening between four & five* oc'k *All hands muster on deck—Make a rush for the* deck pot *in which are kept the scrubbrooms.* [*They*] *weigh about 20 lbs. more or less with a handle between 3 & 4 feet long—. . . .*

For some time past we have been overhauling the ships rigging—as to whales—not more than a dozen have been seen from the mastheads and none of the right sort. . . . From what Mr. Barker the Mate says—I think it must be the intention of the Captain to go after right whales—and leave Sperm whaling till the season is better. Wherever the Skipper chooses to go, all must follow. . . .

November 9th Friday *A little before 6 o'clock this morning heard the cheering cry from mast head "there blows" "there blows"—"there goes flukes"—the Captain was on deck in a moment—and after singing out* Where away & *how far off—jumped into the rigging with his glass—presently the lookout cries again there blows half a dozen times—all is now excitement; a general rush is made to get a sight; when the old man sings out get the boats ready—then there is a confusion; each boats crew rushes to their respective boats, and assist the Boat steerers in preparing the boats for dropping. . . .*

Presently the old skipper sings out haul aback the main yard & lower away—this was done in a twinkling—the boats dropped into the water and manned as quick—the sail is set oars shipped and off we go after the Captain's directions—the whale is down now and we are about half a mile from the ship—presently we see a flag floating from the mainmast truck. The whales are up. We see them from the boat—off we put—gain on them fast—get about three ships length when they lift their flukes and sound again—After having an exciting chase of three, four, or more hours we turn about and go on board disheartened—tired & disgusted—such is the sad history of the first whale we saw, chased & didn't get.

The *Clara Bell* continued to track whales for a month without success, Weir complaining that "With our usual luck, if we keep on this fashion will be obliged to remain out 3 times 3 years to fill ship." But then their fortune changed.

[***December***] ***9th Sunday*** *. . . at 9 A.M. lowered the quarter boats again for a right whale. And Mr. Perry got fast to a noble fellow. We had not much difficulty in working around him but he did throw his flukes about most unmercifully: by noon he was fin up and by 7-1/2 P.M. that monstrous Leviathan could only be remembered by the pieces of blubber about deck and in the blubber room. This was a big whale—the thinnest part of a blanket piece measured about 8 inches. Some of the blubber was two feet deep.*

The right whale is a very dirty mamal compared to others of the same tribe—I have noticed they are covered with small insects very much resembling crabs—about half an inch in diameter. On the end of their nose is a bunch of barnacles about 18 inches wide. This the whalemen call his bonnet—and when you see a whale just rising out of water it has the appearance of a rock—the barnacles are enormous—as much as two inches deep—the boys often roast them and eat them the same as oysters. And many other tid bits do they have when a whale is "trying out": cooking whale lean &c &c &c &c. . . .

30th Sunday *. . . it happened to be my*

midnight trick at the wheel Christmas eve—and if I did not feel bad then I never did and never shall—hard life this, but may get used to it—. . . .

1856 Jan. 1st Tuesday What gay times they will have at home today—I wonder if they'll think of me. I must console myself by imagining they will. Last Tuesday, Christmas Day—was scarcely noticed, in the afternoon we gammed [visited] with the bark Helen Augusta—of Tisbury—Capt. West—19 Mos out—1050 bbls right & sperm—sent a letter home by her.

2nd Wednesday. . . . Raised whales this morning and lowered the quarter boats by 6 oclock—returned with our usual good luck—Caught a "Waugin" a species of sea bird that very much resembles the penguin—This was about the size of a drake. We are now bound for a cruise off the Congo River and St Helena ground [in the South Atlantic] for Sperm Whales—. . . .

March 1st Saturday —Been racing all day with the bark Sacramento and gammed this evening—she is 16 Mos out—500 bbl Sperm—She is a match for us—though if the breeze had been a little stiffer she could scarcely have kept up so well. The rumor afloat is that we are bound direct for St. Helena. It seems we are far enough out of the world now—and for my part I wish I was home again—but we may yet make a good voyage. Cheer up—

12th Wednesday At daylight this morning raised St Helena a little on our lee—dropped the mud hook a little before 10 oclock—among about 20 sails—Merchantmen & Whalers—. . . . It seems strange to have the sails furled again and have the vessel be so still upon the water.

25th Tuesday —Weighed anchor between 9 & 10 A.M. Strong S.E.ly breeze blowing with occasional squalls. I have sent two letters home from here—. . . one to Emma in the Ship "Lancer"—. . . . The water boat came alongside and pumped water through a hose into our hold—Painted the ship outside & I do not expect to have any more chances to send letters home, as we are bound direct for the Indian Ocean—to cruise off Fort Dauphin, Madagasr

27th Thursday —. . . While at St Helena each watch had four days liberty—three days of which we each received one dollar from the Captain—upon which large sum we could spree out 24 hours. . . . There was considerable grumbling about the Captain's generosity? Though we must certainly know it is for our benefit to draw lightly during the voyage for a better pocket full on returning home.

I visited Napoleon's tomb—it is about 8 ft by 5 by 10 deep. Merely a walled hole in the earth with a dozen steps to descend to the bottom—it is in a beautiful spot and near by is a delicious spring by which I wish I could at this moment sit down—I have come to the conclusion that the land is the best after all—for at sea you never can be quiet and must put up with all sorts of characters. Give one a home on the solid land—with a fairy to love me—and other dear ones that care for me—that would be happiness—. . . . Ah! The die is cast—and for two weary years & more must I be knocked about at the mercy of wind & wave, before I can think of going home. Then when our vessel does go to that dear land who can tell what happy mortals we shall be—but I am looking too far ahead—we know nothing beyond this minute. God only knows what the future may unfold. He is merciful. . . .

30th Sunday —Five days from St Helena—Had very stormy weather all the while—.

. . . I am again getting used to sea life—and do not care to go on shore again till we reach our own dear native land—so I think now but may alter my opinion—I dare not anticipate too much, for the time is too far off—I wish we could fill up ship and start for home in the shortest possible time.

I had a strange dream of home last night—and of Plancks funeral taking place, at the same time great festivities going on—. . . it is sadly unpleasant for me to have such dreams of home—though it is the second of the kind I have dreamed since leaving—It is seldom I dream unless unwell as I was last night—for all the sleep we can get is too much needed to be frittered away in dreams—Oh! how I wish I could hear from home, what a weight would be lifted from my mind—what joy it would be to see all the dear ones again just as I left them seven months ago—is such a meeting in store for me? My dear father—does he think of me as his son? Oh! how deeply I have wronged you my father—can I ever be forgiven. Oh how I wish I had always spoken with the freedom of a son to you—I might not have been here—but under such circumstances this may all be for the best—

While in St Helena I attended church—and O what happiness it was to be again in the house of God—after so long a separation from religious service—Those moments I think were the happiest I have had since we sailed—Our dear little Church is often before me in my day dreams of home & the Hudson—many a wondering thought do I give as to who is there and who not—but my thoughts are not enough to satisfy the craving desire to know something of those at West Point—I anxiously await more substantial intelligence and hope but a few months will bring relief—. . . .

[April] 2nd Wednesday . . . All my spare time in a watch below is employed in sewing patches upon my clothes—for there is no disgrace in wearing patches at sea—I wish my sisters could see me in my whaling rig—they'd laugh some, I'll wager—In the course of a few months, I presume my garments will be a mass of rags & patches, and I don't know but it would pay to keep one pair of pants to present to Barnum or some such notorious humbug—. . . .

4th Friday . . . The old man cracks on all sail, in order to loose no time—. . . .

This morning (being my watch below) I am engaged in making a bed quilt of calico and strips of blanket—in preparation for cold & comfortless times that we expect off the Cape [Of Good Hope]—. . . . In the evening the Captain dealt out some tobacco, the best Albany oak-leaf can't compare with it—I got four pounds. . . .

9th Wednesday Set taught the Main, Main to gall't, main topmast & royal stays—steering full & by with a stiff breeze and all sail set—I know what a beautiful sight it is to see a vessel skimming the water with all sail set; often have I watched them (years gone by) from our parlour windows; it was a great pleasure for me then,—and what would I not give to be in sight of those scenes of my childhood. . . .

10th Thursday Started the sewing society again, stitch, stitch—patch on patch is all the rage—here are half the ships crew below, going it hammer & tongs with their needles—Here is where I am learning famous lessons in economy; with all sorts of trades, coblering, barberizing, washing, tailoring—with probably many others that do not occur to my mind at present—a whaler might well be called—Jack at all trades—for there is a little of every imaginable thing done on board a whale-ship.

It was Friday the 3rd day of August 1855 that I left Cold Spring for the last time. To go to sea was the last thought that entered my head that morning, but how little did I know myself—I think I & Myself shall be better acquainted on my return—should God see fit to allow it.

11th Friday —. . . I amused myself while pacing the deck last night in thinking over all my lady friends—I wonder if that one whom I looked upon as my star still shines for me. . . .

16th Wednesday Last Monday . . . Mr. Barker the Mate struck a large porpoise, from the Martingale guys—which we hauled on deck, stripped [off] his blubber and hung upon the main stay in a short time—Porpoise flesh is considered by some a delicacy—we eat it for a change—it tastes very much like veal, but is not so firm and is of a dark color—the oil tried from the blubber is used in the binnacle lamps, as it gives a remarkably clear light while burning. . . .

17th Thursday *Mr. Barker lowered for* [*a*] *Sun-fish—but we lost sight of him shortly after the boat left the ship. I would like very much if we could get one—the oil from the liver is said to be excellent for rheumatism and is used for many medicinal purposes.*
18th Friday *Scudding like a sea bird before the wind—with all the square sails set—.*
. . . At our present rate of sailing we'll soon be right off the South point of the Cape—

It is now 4 P.M.. The wind has increased so much that the fore-top-sail was double reefed—and when a huge sea lifts us—our good bark seems fairly to fly—so lightly does she float—anyway if she don't fly the spray does—. . . . Clara *staggers like a drunken man, you are tossed here, there & everywhere, like a ball in a box; with the pots, pans, spoons, chests &c &c—you cannot resist dancing a jig—on deck it is touch & go—the seas washing over continually keep the decks so slippery that it is dangerous moving about, for they are inclined nearly fourty degrees every few seconds—*

Life lines have been rigged aft and the watch on deck is obliged to stop there and keep out of danger—. . . .
20th Sunday *Eight months from home today—. . . . Just past the extreme point of the Cape—and upon the verge between the Indian & Atlantic Oceans—We are fast moving to the scene of operation; the whaling ground—with wonderful expectations as to filling the ship in one season.*

One sail in sight this afternoon, bound for Atlantic shores—Another sail this morning off our weather bow—on the same tack as we.
21st Monday *. . . Many and many a weary league am I now from those I love—and O what a life for me to lead, among an ungodly set of men—where there is nothing but coarse & immoral language used—It is something I can never get accustomed to—And yet I have to put up with it for at least two years more—*

But I am undergoing a rather rigid schooling, which cannot soon be forgotten. I regret being secluded from society, and such refinement as I have formerly been accustomed to—far beyond everything—I must improve my time in every possible way—Mentally, Morally & physically—. . . .
22nd Tuesday *. . . At noon running under double-reefed topsails—Wind increased to a gale—by sunset we were staggering under a foresail & close reef'd Main topsail. The seas were pretty heavy, and continually washed our decks—Everything, fore & aft was well soaked & washed with salt water—several seas pitched over us scarcely sprinkling the decks. The order*

Weir's diary sketches: "Evening Exercise"

"Got fast to a noble fellow"

"Entering Indian Ocean"

"Sports of Whalemen"

"Striking Attitude"

"Dog Watch"

of the day at such times is turn in wet & turn out smoking—. . . .

24th Thursday *—. . . By 7 P.M. we were scudding along with incredible speed, full 14 knots—amidst a sheet of foam and a deluge of rain; It seems madness to rush along so—but there was no alternative. We were now under close reefed Main top sail—and a bellying foresail—What would a landsman think to see us now—the sea running awfully high—*

For a moment we would be lifted upon the summit of a great sea, amidst a cloud of spray—anon we were dropped between two mountain heaps—where it was almost a calm—and all our headway apparently gone. Look up—see that towering billow astern—we shall be engulfed—but no—the Mass of water would rush on—our good bark would mount high upon its top—and again give a plunge, and start ahead like a frightened deer—

Occasionally during the night the gale would lull a little and our good barque would then be plunging and rolling at a fearful rate—The seas rushing by tons over our decks—It was worth ones life to let go a hands grasp from the rigging for a moment—Again the gale would come upon us with redoubled fury—Making the sea look like driven snow—and lifting showers of water from the crests of the waves—which fell upon us like heavy rain. One may imagine a sailors life is a cheerless one in such times, and so it is to some—but not so to me—for I love to be on deck and watch the sea & sky and hear the Almighties voice in the storm—it makes us feel that we are actually in the Great Presence of the Omnipotent. It serves to remind all that God is still there and watching over them. The sea is His and He made it. How little we think so—And yet we know that His slightest thought could send us all to destruction—could send the Whole Universe—I should think sailors above all men should be christians—because they seem to live in the depths of dangers—and God is eternally saving them from destruction—It is trying to be seperated from the rest of the World—a mere speck upon the bosom of the Ocean. Nothing to be seen around but sea & sky—What an atom is a ship at sea compared with the Universe—And yet God is there. . . .

May 1st Thursday *—This month will be a memorable one at home on account of Emma's Marriage which was set for this time—And a right gay time they were to have—But here am I—far-far away in the Indian Ocean. . . .*

4th Sunday *Yesterday (3rd) spoke & gammed with the bark Isabella [of] N. Bedford. 8 mos from home been in port about 6 weeks ago—in Toula Bay, Madagascar—They sent about 2 dozen terrapins on board of us—and now every turn one takes about the deck he is afoul of them.*

This Morning we raised what the whalemen call a stinker—a large dead whale—bore down for it and found it to be a Finback whale—too long dead to be of good—the sharks appeared to hold a meeting of some kind over the carcass—doubtless in regard to its removal. The birds were not more backward in their addresses. Commenced standing boats-crew watches last night; a sure sign that we are on the whaling ground—For the past 2 days we have been cruising in sight of Mad^gs—This is that far famed sperm whale ground Fort Dauphin—The weather is boisterous—and the coming 3 months are said to be Typhoon season off here—where we shall go now I cannot say—I would not grumble to go home—. . . .

18th Sunday *. . . For the past fortnight we have had very disagreeable weather—and for the past two days we have had a great many heavy rain squalls—accompanied with thunder and lightening—It rained in torrents all this morning watch from 2 till 7 oc'k. My expectations that were once so exalted, are now fast falling below Zero—here have we been 8 months—aye—9 months from home—and have not even seen a sperm whale blow. . . .*

25th Sunday *. . . A few Minutes before 8 oclock Thursday morning we discovered a school of cows & calves off our bow—about 3 miles distant—We are then steering North—We immediately bore off and ran almost due E—head on for the square heads—gradually we neared them, and new life seemed to possess us all by this time—The anticipation of capturing some of those mamals and having glorious sport. The boats were quickly in readiness. And no sooner had the captain given the order to "lower away the boats" than all three boats with their respective crews were in the water quicker'n Jarvis—And now our sail is set and as we are to the windward of the whales it is necessary to observe the strictest silence—each one has peaked his oar & grasped the paddle—and we all tug away with a hearty good will—but the whales seem to anticipate danger and have quickened their speed—*

After chasing for nearly two hours Mr. Perry's boat got fast—and a few minutes after Mr. Welsh's boat was fast securely to a cow—Our boat was a half a mile off at this time but we shortly pulled up—so soon as the other boats got fast we took in our sail—stowed away the paddles and bent to our oars with desperation—soon we were close by the waist boats whale—and now the Mate sung out to Johnson our boatsteerer—"stand up and give it to him" and he did

CONTINUED ON PAGE 61

Top: an Arab of the Comoro Islands
Above: "Our Bully Mate"

The vivid paintings on this and the following pages were made by Charles S. Raleigh, a veteran of thirty years at sea, who turned to art in 1877. Over the next three decades—until failing eyesight forced him to stop painting—he produced some eleven hundred marine canvases. Most of his astonishing output depicted whaling scenes, though Raleigh himself never sailed aboard a whaler. The dramatic incidents and vivid details that enliven his rarely seen paintings were all described to him by retired captains who lived near his New Bedford, Massachusetts, home.

Below: In Going on Sperm Whales, *a harpooner prepares to sink his iron.*

ALL: NEW BEDFORD WHALING MUSEUM

The Gam *shows whaling men from the* Sea Fox, *the* James Allen, *and the* Commodore Allen *breaking the monotony of sea life with a visit.*

Below: A wounded whale might turn on its pursuer and avenge its agony with devastating effect. The occurrence was common enough for Raleigh to title this painting All in a Day's Work. *The unfortunate crewmen are from the bark* Gazelle.

OVERLEAF: *The* George & Susan*—which sailed the world for an amazing seventy-five years—is seen* Getting a Right Whale. *Flags such as that shown sticking from the whale's hulk marked a ship's kills when rival vessels were in the area.*

H

CATALPA

CONTINUED FROM PAGE 52

give it to solid—an instant and the water is white with foam, but the whale dont stop to fight—off he darts—dragging our two boats humming through the water—shortly he slackens his speed—

The Mate is now in the bows—lance in hand—"haul line" he shouts—We soon haul close, and the Mate has darted the lance chock to the socket in leviathan's very vitals—again the water foams—but this time it is red with the blood of the whale—and off he starts, swifter than ever—The line hums around the loggerhead—and the water has to be freely hove upon it—the sparks fly—look out there! Foul line—the tub man cries out—and quicker than thought a whole bunch of line is whisked past every one in the boat—Another bunch flies out this time dislodging several of the crew from their places—The line is now displaced from the chock—and drags across the mates body—soon the whale slackens again and we reset the line—we again haul up and keep close to the whale—the Mate lances him three or four times more—Oh! look out—he is moving his circle—he'll be fin up shortly—look to your oars, men—keep clear of him while he's in his flurry—Now the water foams and flies—stearn off for your lives—we quickly stearn off & look again—the whale is dead—he is fin *up—If all Sperm Whales are as easily captured as this, we won't have much difficulty—it is far different from right whaling for they fight like mad with their enormous flukes—but a square head don't lift his flukes so threateningly—*

When this whale lay alongside before cutting in, I had some leisure to survey him—My first impression was that it was a half-formed work of the creator—but when I thought who made that creature, I could see beauty in every inch of it—Oh how wonderful and curious are all thy works oh thou Creator. . . .

"Meridian—Our Mate"

On June 6 the *Clara Bell* dropped anchor off Port Victoria on Mahé Island, one of the Seychelles group of islands northeast of Madagascar. After a stay of eleven days, during which fresh fruit, vegetables, and meat were taken aboard, she departed to renew the search for sperm whales.

[July] 4th Friday *—. . . This day has been one of a little enjoyment with us—cocoanuts, roast pig—minced pies, soft tack, ginger cake, pepper sauce, Molasses, pepper, rice and pickles, was our bill of fare—quite extensive for sailors—wound up the day by firing salutes with a couple of packs of fire crackers—and a grand consertino given by the Steward and Myself on an old tin pan and a cracked flute—. . . .*

26th Friday *—Bird Island in sight—lying off and on this afternoon—the jolly boat & bow-boat went ashore after eggs—at noon—brought a full boat load on board—as we could obtain them without the slightest difficulty—the island has an area of about a square mile—it is almost barren, a few bushes & many weeds constitute all the verdure—but the great feature is the Myriad of birds & eggs that are upon it—the birds hover about the island like a dense cloud—and it is necessary to walk carefully else you will crush eggs at every step: and it was something of a job to drive the birds out of the way, in order to get their eggs—. . . .*

August 1st Friday *—. . . Saw a very large sword fish this morning, that deadly enemy of the Sperm Whale. That is excepting ourselves and other whalemen—We often see "devil fish" or* diamond *fish as they call them on board here—they put one very much in mind of a mamoth bat or vampure with horns and tusks which look very white—. . . . The shovel-nosed shark is another curious fish—said to be perfectly harmless—though it has a loathsome appearance. The largest kind of shark is the bone shark—he lives upon the same kind of food as the right whale—. . . .*

Cruising near the Equator, in sight of the east coast of Africa, the *Clara Bell* was so beset by foul weather, dead calm, currents, and winds that for more than seven weeks she was unable to make port. Bread and molasses became the food staple for all on board. Finally, on September 26, the whaling ship got close enough to Saddle Island, of the Comoro group, to be towed in. The stay was brief—there was sickness among the Arab residents—but time enough to take on provisions before heading out to the hunting grounds again. Tragedy struck soon afterward.

[October] 26th Sunday *—. . . This afternoon at 1 1/4 o'clock—Johnson a noble young man and friend of all was lost—There was a heavy sea on—at 2 P.M. the martingale guys gave way—and had to be immediately repaired or the loss of our bowsprit & foretop-mast would have followed—A little after four o'clock Johnson was sewing the guys together just abaft the martingale—When the Mate sung out to the Captain telling him all was right—we braced forward the main yards and as the ships head came to the wind—she met three heavy seas, causing her to pitch heavily—twice Johnson was dashed several feet beneath the water—but he still kept his hold against the awful pressure—the third time he was madly forced under & the great power of the waters was too much for him—he was dragged from his hold—ropes, and*

In Weir's "Too Late," a whale dives.

"Small fry"

"Heave 'Pull"

"Cutting In"

"Stripping blubber off Blackfish Whales"

"Extracting Ivory"

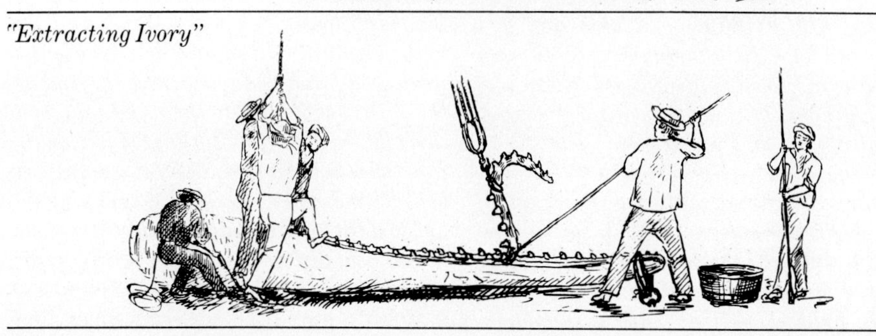

every available thing were hove to him—a boat was cut away & manned but all too late—The startling cry of man overboard thrilled all to their very hearts core—what could be done in such weather—the seas running so high—the ship dashing madly through the water—

Oh! what feeling filled my breast—as I rushed to clear the boat and help save him who was overboard in such a gale; I thought of my wronged parent—of my present situation—the many sins upon my heart—Oh! What happiness it must be to be a christian—and always be ready to die—I have taken this event in its true light as a warning for us all. O! that I could think more of God; so merciful to all sinful mortals—Oh! God give me that strength to love & fear Thee eternally—. . . .

Weir was appointed by the captain to take Johnson's place as boatsteerer (harpooner) of his small whaleboat. He assumed the new assignment, vowing to "strive to do my best for the voyage."

November 16th Sunday *Sail in sight. proved to be the J. Dawson 13 mos out 100 bbls Sperm—gammed all the afternoon. At dark luffed to the wind heading NNE—wind E & N—at 6 1/2 A.M. Land in sight. Madagascar—tacked ship—heading E.S.E.—Raised Sperm whales at 10 o'clock this Morning—lowered in company with the John Dawson—boats returned without success—*

23rd Sunday *—At 3 1/2 P/M/ gammed with the bark Massasoit 31 mos out 700 Sperm*

24th Monday *—Stiff breeze & rugged sea—3 sails in sight. At 6 1/4 A.M. raised Sperm whales—lowered about 9 A.M. Waist-boat got fast & was taken to wind'rd smoking—by noon quarter boats came aboard—bearing with the ship—all sail set—at 1 p.m. lowered the quarter boats and chased whales to leeward—Waist boat set signals of distress—Ship also—pulled hard to the rescue & found her stove—Larboard boat got fast & settled the business—by 4 P.M. whale alongside—and a big fellow he is too—*

25th *Commenced cutting in at daybreak—by noon had all in but the head—2 sails seen—*

November 26th Wednesday *Spoke the ship "Martha"—no letters for me—and she is but 6 months from home. but soon we hope to see other & later sails.*

Dec—24th Wednesday *Chasing whales all day—lowered the boats 4 times—before breakfast—after breakfast—after dinner & supper—no success attended our movements—the weather was too good.*

29th Monday *—Gammed with the "H.H.*

Crapo" chock a block—*bound for home shortly. I sent four letters on board—One to . . . Father. . . .*

1857 January 6th Tuesday *—Gammed with the small bark "Acorn" 5 mos from home—No letters, not even for the Captain—What is the Matter?*

7th Wednesday *—Gammed with the United States six months out—as unfortunate as usual—have they forgotten me—I think not.*

11th Sunday *—I've struck my whale—lowered 11 A.M. by 12 o'clock Mr. Barker put me on a noble whale—took him head & head—I got up and gave it to him solid—Whiz—whiz—whiz—it seemed but a moment & all the line was out of one of our tubs—160 fathoms—I hold the turn—he shortly slacks—and again comes up to blow—The Starboard gets fast & within an hour he is fin up—the Waist boat was there with the bomb-lance—but did not have an opportunity to use it. . . .*

12th Monday *—This morning got the case & junk on deck—enormous—talk about your elephants—Mastodons—and Mamoth Monsters of the earth—what are they compared to a Noble Whale—how the land folk would open their eyes to see such a head as this—*

I am 21 years old this day—oh! how the time flies—and these moments can never be recalled—I wish I was somewhere near civilization—I'd feel better satisfied—

To remain here 18 mos more seems awful—but I've battled it so far—why not finish with Gods help—if father could see me now—. . . .

For the next eleven months the *Clara Bell* ranged back and forth across the Indian Ocean hunting whales, sometimes in company with another whaling ship, the *Eugenia.* There was little time for anything but work—hunting whales during daylight hours and often working through the night to render the blubber into oil. The two vessels put into port only when provisions gave out. For Weir, there was scarcely time to record entries in his journal, much less ruminate about his state of mind—or engage in, as he put it, "schrimschawing, or whatever these intolerable whalemen call it." By December, 1857, the *Clara Bell* had been at sea for more than two years without Weir having received a letter from any member of his family, and he was resigned now never to hear from home.

December 9th Wednesday *—. . . We succeeded in sailing upon a noble fellow . . . our good boat fairly flew before the wind—When Barker the Mate sang out "look out for him Wallace" I was up in a moment, . . . picked up my first iron and darted with Might and Main right in the center of Leviathans side—the second harpoon was burried in the bunch of his neck, in an instant he darted about three ship lengths ahead of our boat rolled over on his back, and worked his old jaw like the lever of a steam engine—at the same time lashing the sea with fury. The Starboard boat now ventured up, and with some difficulty succeeded in getting an iron in to him. When Mr. Whale politely poked his jaw through the boat—making a hole as big as the head of a barrel—*

Never mind says Barker, from our boat, unbend your boats sail & plug it up.

We had to work warily about this customer. After considerable manouvering Mr. Barker darted his lance, and in a moment the whale had our boat in his ponderous jaw and raised high out of water—Crack, crash, crack—we were all tumbled pell-mell into the water—and our boat left a total wreck, bitten to pieces—happily no one was injured. It was now time to look about for the ship—Mr. Perry could give us no help for he was already badly stoven, and could with difficulty keep afloat. There was the Clara Bell a mile off dead to leeward—Beating up, under a stiff topgallant breeze—the men trimmed the sails with a will that day and our noble bark beat up gloriously—soon we saw the Captain lower in the waist boat—but so soon as he came near the whale—who was scribing a circle about us all the time, Mr. Whale put towards him, this was a fix—however Mr. Perry pulled up with his stoven boat—and whilst he attracted the whales notice the captain took us all safely on board and off we started for the ship—leaving Perry alone with the whale; it took but a few minutes to unlash a spare boat from the hurricane house & launch it—oars, shot pins and a spare lance were put into it, and off we started for the fight. Mr. Barker took Mr. Welsh & his bomb battery up on the Starboard side of the whale while the Captain took Mr. Perry up on his Larboard quarter—Perry darted his lance with good effect and at the same moment Welsh fired a bomb lance into him—which performances made his whaleship furious—the flap of his flukes upon the water sounded like artilery—and his jaw came down like a trip hammer. The second lance Mr. Perry threw brought the blood from his spouthole—Mr. Welsh fired three bomb lances into him—when Mr. Whale knocked off the head of his boat, and tossed our notable man with the bomb-gun into the water. His whaleship expired with the day—and by 6 1/2 P.M. we had him tied by the tail.

At sunrise we commenced cutting in. *10 A.M. body in. 11 3/4—junk safe on deck & now for dinner; with a desert of yarns about Taber Tom as the boys call our whale.*

10th Thursday *3 p.m. case safe on deck—and a couple of men burried to their necks in the centre of it, bailing out the spermacetti as though a human life depended upon their exertions—Wouldn't this be a rich scene for the dear ones at home to see—a couple of men burried in a whale head—a delightful situation surely—*

Started the works between 4 & 5 P.M. trying out the head first—6 P.M. sail in sight chasing whales—too late in the evening for us to lower—though the whales could be seen plainly from deck—Hard at work with the fires all night—This morning the barque "Montgomery" close to chasing whales—8 A.M. her boats fast—we lowered & chased for a couple of hours, without success—All hands on deck from sunrise to sunset. 5 1/2 hours rest out of the 24—pleasant and no mistake—the old skipper takes it comfortably & gets well paid for it—but the officers suffer with the sailors—good. . . .

1858 January 1st Friday *. . . Made all sail this morning, a splendid day—the dawning of the New Year; and here we are hard at work coopering on the decks of Clara. Precious few casks I make this day. . . . raised sperm whales—and chased with all sail set till near noon when we lowered away the boats—the whales had gone down, and we were pulling industriously towards a spot where we thought they would rise—when to our surprise a pod of them rose directly under our boat—I grasped the harpoon to heave into the side of a noble big fellow—when I heard the mate crying out in a rather loud whisper "Are you mad man, you'll kill us all," I looked around & here we were almost resting on the flukes of one and the head of another—the slightest prick to any one of a half dozen of whales about us would certainly have been our ruin. I momentarily expected the boat would have been dashed to atoms—there I stood harpoon in hand, and the crew with oars suspended in the air, like so many statues, did not dare move a muscle, when the whales became aware of some danger . . . and all sunk like so many tons of lead: We now breathed freely—. . . .*

The next month seemed the busiest of all. Whale boats were out almost every day, the try works, or rendering furnaces, on deck blazed away during the night, and barrel upon barrel was stowed below. As the month ended, preparations were at last under way for the passage home. But first the *Clara Bell* made port, at St. Augustine Bay, which is situated on the southwest coast of Madagascar.

[February] 2nd Tuesday *...found ourselves in company with three French brigs—two of which are slavers—had to turn to immediately and break out paint &c. Our decks are swarming with natives. This morning set up the bobstays and painted ship outside—rafted 14 casks for water—and now we only await orders from the Prince before we dare to go ashore for anything....*

4th Thursday *...hoisted the water on deck and rolled it forward—in order to bury the ships head & lift the stern to get at [a] leak—Chips [the ship's carpenter] has been up to his armpits in the water working at the leak all the morning. A sail in sight coming in—Went ashore with the captain to get a bullock—and a time we had too. Two tribes of the natives were fighting, popping away at one another with their shooting things. When they had popped off about a keg of powder one party retreated to the hills leaving one dead man upon the field.*

The *Clara Bell* weighed anchor and began her voyage home around the Cape of Good Hope on February 8. The crewmen grumbled now when the wind either turned against them or died down completely, and complained when the captain hove to in order to track down yet another school of whales. By March 11, however, the ship had reached St. Helena, and nine days later the final leg of the journey was begun. As the prospect of returning to his family grew closer to reality, Weir once again became anxious. He was determined now to try to make amends for his behavior at home.

[April] 9th Friday *...Had a long gaze at the North Star last night the sky being clear in that quarter; and what vivid recollections of by gone days it brought before me; how often have I looked upon that star while crafting the noble Hudson between West Point and Cold Spring, or while any where about home and at night, Can I look at that star from that loved place again. I trust it may be so, but I can't anticipate....*

18th Sunday *...Dreaming of home by night & thinking and talking of home by day—and so it is with all the crew.*

But will they—can they ever love me as formerly? If not—no one is to blame but my most willful self—deeds, not words must hereafter mark my life—how shall I face my honored & good father—to obtain his forgiveness is all I shall seek—and my future life must show my gratitude....

19th Monday *...how I should like to walk to Church this afternoon with Em—I wonder if they will think of me this day—well! there is some satisfaction in imagining they will—flattering thought—....*

21st Wednesday *Still steering NW—have not made any more sail yet—3 sails in sight—3 P.M., a schooner running across our bows—we hauled aback, and lowered a boat for news—proved to be the "Charm" from Phila. 10 days out—they tossed us a package of papers, which proved a grand treat—and serves to make us realize that we are actually drawing near home—....*

22nd Thursday *Steering NW with light SEly breeze—Under top gallant sails—Oh! dear! how can the Old Man [the captain] keep us reduced to this short sail with so light a wind....*

24th Saturday *Steering NNW. With a Villanous 3 knot breeze. Sailors muttering & growling. Painted the Larboard side of the ship...touched up scientifically here & there on the inside of the bulwarks.... Scraped & varnished the lash rail & spanker boom—scraped all the masts—Clara begins to look new indeed. Barstow the owner will congratulate himself on having left his petted craft in the hands of such a skipper....*

27th Tuesday *—...Hurrah we have a smacking breeze—and it is still on the increase—as it has been all night—Made a new spanker-out haul-block for the heel of the spanker boom, the last job I hope to do this voyage—....*

May 2nd Sunday *Wind from SW. Excellent weather. Head WNW fresh breeze—but not fair enough.... Our passage through the waters is like a comet—there is such a brilliant train of phosphorescent light behind us—it contrasts brilliantly with the surrounding darkness, this illumination does not appear like the general lights of the waters—it has a ghostly look—a bluish white—while elsewhere there is a warm pink or yellow tinge—*

Between 10 P.M. & 1 A.M. the water around the ship was splendid to look at—it flashed & sparkled far beneath the surface, looking like so many twinkling stars in the heavens—

About 2 hours before the Moon rose—we had a sight which brought many home recollections to our minds—it was the Aurora Borealis—Everything now indicates our close proximity to our native land—to our glorious home—We see the North Star almost as high in the heavens as they do at home—And there is not more than 6 or 8 minutes variations in the time compared with home—hurrah—we are blessed indeed....

3rd Monday *...This morning took all the whaling craft from the boats and stowed it below—stripped all the chafing gear from the rigging &c—2 schooners in sight but where is the land. We suffer with the cold—that thermometer stands 50°—they'll laugh at us at home—but if we can actually get there, let them laugh & we will join in with a hearty good will....*

May 4th Tuesday *Steering NE. Moderate breeze—fine weather, clear and cold—set the main royal at 1 P.M. 2 P.M. set the fore royal—3 P.M. set the fore top mast & lower studding sails—4 P.M. set the main top gallant studding s'ls. Breeze dying away—what shall we do? The land ought to be in sight by our reconing—curious navigation this—The Old Man seems to be perfectly indifferent as regards getting home—he must be case hardened or else he is putting these contrary actions upon himself to tantalize us.*

5 1/2 P.M. Joyful news the reviving cry of Land ho! has been uttered—and three hearty cheers made the welkin ring again—My pulse beats warmer, and though I have 8 hours to watch on deck this night—it will be done cheerfully, for I feel it to be the last weary watch for me to hold—The wind is quite light but fair, and increasing somewhat

7 1/2 p.m. dark, raised Montauk light—

8 P.M. Took soundings—Made 35 fathoms—tacked ship & kept lookouts at the mast head all night—in order to keep the light in sight—I had one dreary cold hour to spend there myself with the second mate continually disturbing me while thinking of home—he talked about his wife & child—but I couldn't listen to him—for I had my own thoughts for better company—.... At Midnight the ship Huntsville was close to—they sent a boat alongside for a short gam and comparison of reckoning—

The weather is villanously cold—enough so to keep up all in an uncomfortable state—4 A.M. daybreak—Made all sail—6 A.M. 6 sails in sight. Mostly schooners. 6 1/2 Pilot boat Relief bearing down to us—hove too with main yard aback—and received the Pilot—braced forward and steered N! Wind light from W. several islands in sight—Martha's Vinyard, Gayhead—right ahead—Rhode I off Larboard beam—

7 P.M. We touched the wharf and I touched the shore—pure bona fide American land hurrah—

We are now safely moored at one of the N. Bedford wharves—it is glorious to think of. But I am thankful—We had a favorable breeze to come in with, and the pilot took us chock into the wharf—

9 P.M. I have just returned from a stroll on solid Yankee land.

How shall I face my dear father. I shall go directly to him—and tell him all—I trust God will yet give me strength of resolution to reform.—

Weir's Clara Bell *homeward bound*

Epilogue

Did Weir's father forgive him? We can only guess, because Weir's journal ends without telling us. However, it appears likely that all turned out well. He returned to the sea during the Civil War, serving under Farragut at the battle of Mobile Bay. He also was a war correspondent and illustrator for *Harper's*. A construction engineer by profession, he worked at one time for the Croton Water Works in New York and later as a consultant to the Union Subway Construction Company, dying finally in Montclair, New Jersey, shortly after his sixty-ninth birthday, in 1905.

For further reading, see Prof. Hareven's chapter, "Child Labor," in Children and Youth In America, *Vol. 2 (Harvard University Press, 1971).*

DR. GEORGE WASHINGTON CARVER
UNITED
STATES
POSTAGE
3¢

George Washington Carver and the Peanut

New Light on a Much-Loved Myth

by Barry Mackintosh

The election of a peanut-growing President has evoked much journalistic analysis of his rural Southern roots. One political observer credited an earlier peanut personality at a black school not far from Plains, Georgia, with "a more important role in Carter's destiny than latter-day supporters like Andrew Young or Maynard Jackson or Martin Luther King, Sr." Writing in the Washington *Post*, Douglass Cater went on to recall how "George Washington Carver, born a slave, set up the primitive laboratory at the Tuskegee Institute to become 'the father of chemurgy' and 'the Peanut Wizard,' working in tandem with the boll weevil to rid the South of its dependence on the one-crop cotton economy.... Carver demonstrated that the lowly 'goober' not only could enrich soil exhausted by cotton growing ... but held myriad commercial uses. Spurred by Dr. Carver, peanut farming transformed the economy of Sumter County and lifted the Carter family out of its hard-scrabble existence."

George Washington Carver was among the best-known American figures of this century and perhaps the single most renowned black American of his time. A white society unaccustomed to ascribing brilliance to blacks acclaimed him a genius. "Professor Carver has taken Thomas Edison's place as the world's greatest living scientist," Henry Ford announced near the end of Carver's life; Senator Champ Clark of Carver's native Missouri called him "one of the foremost scientists of all the world for all time." Upon Carver's death in 1943, Congress passed and President Roosevelt signed legislation making his birthplace a national monument—an honor previously granted only Washington and Lincoln. Last spring Carver was enshrined in the Hall of Fame for Great Americans in New York City.

Carver's scientific discoveries and his transformation of Southern agriculture can truly be described as legendary—in the fullest sense. For Carver was both less and more than he seemed. What he did was less important than what he was and the larger purposes his existence served for blacks and whites alike.

George Carver began life sometime during the Civil War as the property of Moses Carver, a southwestern Missouri farmer of moderate wealth. "My sister, mother and myself were ku clucked and sold in Arkansaw," he once wrote of a kidnapping by border-raiding bushwhackers during his infancy; his owner gave a horse in payment for his recovery, according to later accounts. The orphaned child stayed on the Carver farm near Diamond Grove for a decade after emancipation, then left to seek schooling in nearby Neosho. During these years he developed the love of plants that would remain with him ever after. "Day after day I spent in the woods alone in order to collect my floral beauti[e]s and put them in my little garden...," he later recalled. "... strange to say all sorts of vegetation seemed to thrive under my touch until I was styled the plant doctor, and plants from all over the county would be brought to me for treatment." Painting and music were additional subjects of what he called his "inordinate desire for knowledge."

Moving on from place to place, supporting himself by laundering, cooking, and other odd jobs, Carver completed his secondary education, worked briefly as a Kansas City stenographer, tried homesteading in western Kansas, and in 1890 enrolled at Simpson College in Iowa to study art. But his botanical interest triumphed: he transferred to the Iowa Agricultural College at Ames and there earned his B.S. degree in 1894. Remaining as an assistant botanist on the experiment station staff, he obtained an M.S. in agriculture two years later.

Professor James Wilson, who would serve as Secretary of Agriculture under Presidents McKinley, Roosevelt, and Taft, took Carver under his wing at Ames. In turn, the student transmitted his botanical enthusiasm to another, much younger, future Agriculture Secretary: Henry A. Wallace later fondly remembered "many a Saturday afternoon collecting plant specimens in the woods and fields about Ames" with Carver.

When the state of Alabama enacted legislation to support an agricultural school and experiment station for blacks at Tuskegee Institute in February, 1897, Tuskegee's able principal, Booker T. Washington, was prepared. The previous April Washington had asked Carver to head the new program. "Of course it has always been the one great ideal of my life to be of the greatest good to the greatest number of 'my people' possible," Carver responded before accepting, "and to this end I have been preparing my life for these many years; feeling as I do that this line of education is the key to unlock the golden door of freedom to our people."

Carver's enthusiasm for agricultural education had cooled somewhat by the time he arrived at Tuskegee in the fall of 1896. "I do not expect to teach for many years," he informed the school's finance committee, "but will quit as soon as I can trust my work to others, and engage in my brush work, which will be of great honor to our people showing to what we may attain...." Nor was agricultural training popular with Tuskegee students, many of whom saw schooling as a means of escaping the farm. When the agriculture department graduated only two students in 1910, a dissatisfied Booker Washington removed Carver from charge and made him head of a new Department of Research.

Carver continued teaching for some time on a limited basis, but without distinction. "There is criticism among teachers and students to the effect that in your teaching you do not pursue a regular, logical and systematic course, that you jump about from one subject to another without regard to the course of study laid down in the catalogue," Washington warned him in 1912. "Some of your students are getting rather restless."

Carver enjoyed little more success at overseeing the school farms, which Washington expected to be model paying operations. John Washington, Booker's brother, questioned Carver's superintendency in 1902: "The fences, gates, etc. are not kept up, and, as a rule, seem to have no attention, until somebody not connected directly with the Agricultural Department takes ahold of the matter." When Booker Washington found fifty bushels of sweet potatoes rotting in the basement of the Agricultural Building he rebuked Carver sternly: "It is not very becoming to be teaching agriculture on one floor and on the next floor have such an exhibition as these potatoes presents of the want of proper methods of caring for agricultural products." G. Lake Imes, a long-time faculty colleague, recalled Carver as one who "did not fit very well into the college routine."

Carver was happier with experimental work, which became his chief concern after 1910. The Tuskegee Experiment Station served as a testing ground for crop varieties and fertilizers. In the laboratory he analyzed soil, feed, well water, and other materials submitted from the school and its vicinity. Because the rural poor around Tuskegee could ill afford commercial feed and fertilizer, he demonstrated the value of substitutes like acorns for feeding hogs and swamp muck for enriching croplands. Staffed by blacks and directed to a black farm population largely unaffected by progressive agricultural practices, the Tuskegee station addressed an important need in Alabama's black belt.

Carver attempted to reach a wider audience with the experiment station bulletins, leaflets, and circulars that appeared under his name from 1898 to his death. They contained little that was new. Much of his message was summarized in a leaflet distributed by the institute before his arrival: "Do not plant too much cotton, but more corn, peas, sugar-cane, sweet-potatoes etc., raise hogs, cows, chickens, etc." The extent of Carver's efforts to broadcast such advice to rural blacks was unprecedented. Yet the actual impact of his bulletins and other extension work was moderate at best. Whatever success he had in uplifting the rural poor could scarcely have accounted for the nationwide prominence he would attain. That came through his identification with the peanut.

A few years after his arrival at Tuskegee, Carver raised a small quantity of Spanish peanuts at the experiment station. Recognizing the soil-building and nutritional values of the legume, he mentioned it in a 1905 bulletin, *How to Build Up Worn Out Soils*. Eleven years later he focused on the crop in another, *How to Grow the Peanut and 105 Ways of Preparing It for Human Consumption*, in which he credited recipe books and other sources. Not until the postwar years did he assume an innovative role with peanuts. In 1919 he wrote a Birmingham peanut-processing firm about a milk substitute he had just produced from the plant: "... it is without doubt the most wonderful product that I have yet been able to work out, and I see within it, unlimited possibilities."

Learning of Carver's work, the United Peanut Associations of America asked him to appear at their convention in Montgomery in September, 1920. Peanut growers, millers, and manufacturers faced with declining prices had formed the organization to lobby for a protective tariff on imported peanuts. Carver's presentation on "The Possibilities of the Peanut" was enthusiastically received despite "doubts lingering in the minds of the audience as to the advisability of having one of the negro race come before them...," according to a peanut trade journal. "When the time comes when this question must be threshed out before the American Congress," Alabama Congressman Henry B. Steagall announced in reference to the tariff, "I propose to see that Professor Carver is there in order that he may instruct them a little about peanuts, as he has done here on this occasion."

Carver's appearance before the House Ways and Means Committee in January, 1921, launched his national identity as "the peanut man." Some of the congressmen, patronizing him as "uncle" and "brother," greeted Carver as an amusing diversion, but he held the committee's interest well over his allotted time. Again he based his presentation on a great diversity of products that he demonstrated or described, including candy, ice cream flavoring, livestock feed, and ink.

In these appearances Carver was publicizing peanut values and product possibilities already known if not universally appreciated. An 1896 bulletin of the U.S. Department of Agriculture, *Peanuts: Culture and Uses*, had discussed the legume's worth in restoring nitrogen to the soil, its nutritional excellence, and the uses of peanuts and peanut oil in candies, soapmaking, flour, soups, salad dressing, muffins, cattle feed, griddlecakes, and other products and processes. The Agriculture Department had issued another comprehensive bulletin on peanuts in 1909, and its 1917 *Yearbook* had promoted the crop as a wartime substitute.

Carver did not explicitly claim that he had personally discovered all the peanut attributes and uses he cited, but he said nothing to prevent his audiences from drawing the inference. "I have just begun with the peanut," he told the House committee. Thereafter he displayed an ever-growing quantity of peanut

LIBRARY OF CONGRESS

BETTMANN ARCHIVE

BROWN BROTHERS

Carver the teacher and scientist (clockwise from top left): overseeing student work in the classroom at the Tuskegee Institute (Carver is second from the right); posed with a soil sample from Tuskegee's experimental fields; and working alone in his laboratory.

Carver the "Peanut Wizard" with some of the many products he developed from the humble goober
BROWN BROTHERS

products at exhibits and personal appearances throughout much of the country and wrote about such intriguing new discoveries as "peanut nitroglycerine" in the *Peanut Journal,* issued by the Southwestern and Southeastern Peanut Associations.

When pressed for an accounting of his peanut products in 1937, Carver balked. "There are more than 300 of them," he wrote. "I do not attempt to keep a list, as a list today would not be the same tomorrow, if I am allowed to work on that particular product. To keep a list would also give the Institute a great deal of trouble, as people would write wanting to know why one list differs from another. For this reason we have stopped sending out lists."

After his death the Carver Museum, which he had helped create at Tuskegee, credited him with developing 287 peanut commodities. One hundred twenty-three were foods and beverages, 68 were paints or dyes, and the rest were livestock foods, cosmetics, medicinal preparations, and miscellaneous uncategorized items. The catalog was inflated by much near duplication: among the individual entries were bar candy, chocolate-coated peanuts, and peanut chocolate fudge; all-purpose cream, face cream, face lotion, and hand cream; thirty cloth dyes, nineteen leather dyes, and seventeen wood stains. Many items were clearly not original with Carver—even "salted peanuts" was on the list (though peanut butter was not). Nor could the efficacy of every preparation, such as a "face bleach and tan remover," be taken for granted. Since Carver left no formulas for these products other than a single patented peanut cosmetic, later investigators were unable to evaluate or confirm his production of many of them.

Along with the peanut Carver championed the sweet potato, a nutritional complement also well suited to Southern soils. Man could live by the peanut and sweet potato alone, he asserted, for together they constituted a balanced ration. Again he publicized the crop's potential in quantitative terms. "The sweet potato products number 107 up to date," he told the congressional committee during his peanut presentation. "I have not finished working with them yet."

Working almost entirely alone, Carver was uncommunicative about his laboratory procedures. A visiting chemist from nearby Auburn University found that he evaded all questions about how his products were made. G. Lake Imes recalled as "enigmatic" his replies to inquisitive visitors to his laboratory. Robert L. Vann, a black journalist, asked him if he had recorded the formulas for his many discoveries. "To my amazement," Vann reported, "Dr. Carver looked at me and smiled and said, 'I have all of these formulas, but I have not written them down yet.' "

What explanation of his scientific achievements Carver did offer was not calculated to satisfy other scientists. Speaking in 1924 at the Marble Collegiate Church in New York, he declared that he never used books in his work and depended on divine revelation for his product ideas and methods. In later addresses he often repeated his laboratory conversations with "Mr. Creator," who told him what to do.

Although he was often acclaimed for the widespread practical application and influence of his work in agriculture and industry, Carver avoided discussing specifics here as well. In reality, neither peanuts nor sweet potatoes were employed significantly in any new application Carver discovered or suggested. Peanuts continued to go almost entirely into confections and baked goods, peanut butter, and oils. Because most of the nonstandard products created by Carver could be made more easily from other substances, they were essentially curiosities.

Nor did Carver play a significant role in converting Southern farmlands from cotton to peanuts. Despite his widely publicized efforts to promote peanut production and consumption, the greatest increase in the crop preceded his identification with it.

As early as 1909 the chief of the Agriculture Department's Bureau of Plant Industry remarked that the peanut was rapidly becoming an important farm crop throughout the South. Annual American production had climbed from 3,500,000 bushels to 19,500,000 bushels in the twenty years after 1889. When output rose to over 40,000,000 bushels in 1916 the department called the phenomenon "one of the striking developments that have taken place in the agriculture of the South."

Carver's peanut bulletin, *How to Grow the Peanut,* did not appear until that year, and not until the next decade was he prominently associated with the crop. By then peanut production was actually declining from its 1917 peak. Alabama's 1917 output was not reached again until the mid-1930's. It is unlikely that Carver bore much responsibility for this eventual recovery; he observed in a personal letter in 1933 that the farmers of his own county were raising few peanuts. Clearly his influence, both local and regional, was limited.

How, then, did this man of modest, unspectacular achievement become the scientific wizard and agricultural revolutionary known to his and later generations? The progress of the Carver myth may be traced in the writings of journalists, popular biographers, publicists, politicians, and professional historians from the early 1920's to the present.

It took root in 1921 when newspapers across the nation carried accounts of Carver's congressional appearance. It attained full development a decade later with the publication of "A Boy Who Was Traded for a Horse" in *The American Magazine* of October, 1932. Author James Saxon Childers gave Carver full credit for increasing peanut production after the boll weevil invasion, then for stimulating demand by developing peanut products and markets. Carver received hundreds of letters in response to the article, many requesting help with personal problems.

Carver's popular appeal increased with his advancing years. His mail soared again after the *Reader's Digest* condensed the Childers article in February, 1937. *Life* followed in March with a picture story naming him "one of the great scientists of the U.S." Later that year the *New York Times* praised his "300 useful products" from the peanut and "more than 100 products of varying human values" from sweet potatoes. These discoveries, the *Times* declared shortly before Carver's death, had "memorably improved the agriculture of the South."

"The world of science has lost one of its most eminent figures . . . ," President Franklin D. Roosevelt said of Carver's passing on January 5, 1943. "All mankind is the beneficiary of his discoveries in the field of agricultural chemistry." Senator Harry S Truman, testifying a month later for the bill to make Carver's birthplace a national monument, declared that "the scientific discoveries and experiments of Dr. Carver have done more to alleviate the one-crop agricultural system in the South than any other thing that has been done in the history of the United States."

The only full Carver biography approaching objectivity appeared the year of its subject's death. Rackham Holt's *George Washington Carver,* recognizing Carver's products as "not revolutionary in themselves," held him most valuable as a publicist. But the book's admiring, romantic tone perpetuated his existing image. An enthusiastic *New York Times* review by Vincent McHugh, subtitled "A Study in Genius," erroneously credited Carver with originating dehydrated foods.

Later writers scaled new heights of fiction. In Melvin T. Rothwell's *George Washington Carver, A Great Scientist* (1944), it was said that Carver had "stepped out of the heart of the lowly peanut into the heart of humanity . . . ," and that his success was due to "a beneficent Creator who whispered secrets into his ebony ear." Ten years later the noted black author Langston Hughes published *Famous American Negroes,* and, apparently unaware that Carver kept no laboratory records, cited his "formulas in agricultural chemistry that enriched the entire Southland, indeed the whole of America and the world."

The fullest and most widely circulated recent exposition of the Carver legend came in 1966 with Lawrence Elliott's *George Washington Carver: The Man Who Overcame,* condensed in the *Reader's Digest* prior to publication. According to Elliott, Carver led much of Alabama to plant peanuts prior to the First World War before sufficient demand existed for the crop. "So engrossed had he been in staving off the evils of the one-crop system, so successful was he in promoting the peanut, that almost alone he had created a monster as cruel and unforgiving as the weevil itself." Pressed by unhappy farmers, including an old widow "who timidly knocked on Dr. Carver's laboratory door" to ask what to do with her surplus, he retired alone to his laboratory to commune with God and discover the first of "well over 300" peanut products, thereby saving the South from poverty. "By the time he died . . . scores of factories had been built to make them, and their range staggered the mind."

Professional historians and other academics, often scornful of popular writers, were not immune to the myth. In *A History of the South,* published in 1936, historian William B. Hesseltine assigned to Carver "leading rank as an industrial scientist" for his many discoveries. A 1949 book from the University of North Carolina Press, Edward J. Dies' *Titans of the Soil,* credited Carver with the establishment of major business enterprises. Historian Edgar A. Toppin's 1971 *Biographical History of Blacks in America Since 1528* held that "George Washington Carver freed the South from dependence on cotton by developing hundreds of uses for peanuts and sweet potatoes." The current *Encyclopedia Americana* and to a lesser extent the *Britannica* reflect the myth in their Carver entries.

Despite their assertions of his scientific wizardry and profound influence on agriculture and industry, most popular accounts have treated Carver's professional accomplishments superficially. The man himself—careless of money, devout, humble—was the main attraction.

"He combines all the picturesque quaintness of the antebellum type of darkey, the mind of an amazing scientific genius, and the soul of a dreamer," a 1923 article in the *Atlanta Journal* related. "And his career . . . is no less picturesque." For those who found a black genius difficult to accept, the *Journal* offered an explanation: "Professor Carver's nose, distinctly Arabic in type, hints of far-off ancestors who were possibly Egyptian, rather than African . . . ."

Much was made of Carver's unconcern for wealth. Actually, he became involved in at least four commercial ventures, obtained two patents for pigments in addition to that for his peanut cosmetic, and granted over $60,000 to a foundation in his name at the close of his life. But his simple attire and habits and the limited nature and productivity of his ventures led most writers to ignore or deny his commercial activities. "He would permit no patents to be taken out on his discoveries, allow no commercialization of his name," declared Congresswoman Clare Boothe Luce on the fourth anniversary of his death.

Carver's religious nature was another among his appealing qualities. A devout Christian, he led Bible classes at Tuskegee and spent much time in prayer. His attribution of his success to God made him a popular subject for inspirational books and tracts.

"His most notable characteristic, aside from the great mental capacity which marks him as a genius, is his deep humility," the *Montgomery Advertiser* reported in a 1929 front-page feature titled "Negro Genius Shows 'Way Out' for Southern Farmers."

Carver's physical appearance was nothing if not humble, an image he enhanced by his devotion to old, worn clothing. Biographers eagerly seized upon his stereotypical "uncle" aspect as a foil to his brilliance, as in Hermann Hagedorn's depiction of "a stooped old colored man in a saggy alpaca coat shuffling through the dust of an Alabama road."

The journalists and other popular writers who embroidered on the man and his deeds for a receptive public must receive primary credit for the Carver myth. They were abetted by manufacturers of peanut products, whom Carver served as a living "Mr. Peanut," and by Tuskegee Institute, in need of another prominent human symbol after Booker T. Washington's death in 1915. But the man himself played no small part in the outcome.

Carver's role was less one of active deception than passive complicity. In his presentations he blurred the distinction between creative discovery of new chemical syntheses and the production of items already known or requiring no scientific originality. Nor did he attempt to correct erroneous claims by others about him and his work. At best, he issued seemingly modest protestations. "How I wish I could measure up to half of the fine things this article would have me be," he wrote to one author.

While laymen lacked the knowledge to see through the legend, most of those better qualified to appraise Carver's contributions lacked the desire. Responding to an inquiry about Carver's work in 1937, an Agriculture Department official hedged: "Dr. Carver has without doubt done some very interesting things—things that were new to some of the people with whom he was associated, but a great many of them, if I am correctly informed, were not new to other people. . . . I am unable to determine just what profitable application has been made of any of his so-called discoveries. I am writing this to you confidentially and without an opportunity to make further investigation and would not wish to be quoted on the subject."

In 1961 the National Park Service, seeking an evaluation of Carver's achievements for its interpretive programs at the George Washington Carver National Monument, commissioned a study by the University of Missouri's Department of Agricultural Chemistry. The memorandum transmitting the report to Washington reflected concern about the findings: "While Professors Carroll and Muhrer are . . . careful to emphasize Carver's excellent qualities, their realistic appraisal of his 'scientific contributions' . . . is information which must be handled very carefully as far as outsiders are concerned. To put it plainly, it seems to us that individuals or organizations who are inclined to be rather militant in their approach to racial relationships might take offense at a study which superficially purports to lessen Dr. Carver's stature. . . . Our present thinking is that the report should not be published, at least in its present form, simply to avoid any possible misunderstandings."

Fear of stirring racial sensitivities by treating Carver candidly helped perpetuate the myth. But how to account for its widespread acceptance in the first place? As Richard Bardolph has observed in *The Negro Vanguard*, ". . . no white scientist with precisely the same achievements would have been called a 'wizard' or 'the greatest industrial chemist in the world.' " Clearly, Carver's race and the purpose he served as a black achiever were essential to his fame.

At a time when few of their number gained national recognition, black Americans had an obvious stake in the legend. For them Carver was a much-needed success symbol—another sign that blacks could stand on an equal footing with whites. The respect attained by one like Carver, they could hope, would extend in some measure to the race as a whole.

But the mass media most responsible for Carver's reputation were governed by and directed to white Americans, including those indifferent or hostile to black advancement. Without white promotion and acceptance the legend would hardly have flourished.

Not surprisingly, the stake most whites had in the myth differed from that of most blacks. By placing a token black on a pedestal, whites of varying persuasions could deny or atone for prejudice against blacks as a class. For Southern whites, the presence of a black achiever among them could prove that their society was not oppressive to blacks as such; those who failed to achieve could only blame themselves. Finally, a black achiever of the right sort could set a suitable example for others of the race.

Booker T. Washington had been the right sort of black achiever for most whites. They acclaimed his advocacy of industrial education and self-help for blacks and his outward accommodation to the Southern social order. In some ways Carver was even more appealing. Unlike Washington, who occasionally stepped across the color line and worked undercover for black rights, Carver was wholly apolitical. "Rising or falling," he wrote philanthropist George Peabody, "I believe is practically inherent within the individual. . . . I believe in the providence of God working in the hearts of men, and that the so-called Negro problem will be satisfactorily solved in His own good time, and in His own way."

White Southerners found Carver's adherence to the rules and customs of segregation exemplary. When two nonconforming white visitors to Tuskegee asked him to join them for dinner, he excused himself. In 1923, *Success Magazine*, which dubbed him "Columbus of the Soil," approvingly noted how he had "deferentially remained in the background until all of the white men had been heard" by the Ways and Means Committee.

His field of work was another point in his favor. Agriculture was a suitably humble occupation; in choosing to work with the "lowly" peanut, Carver showed that he knew his place vocationally as well as socially. And as a scientist who credited his work to divine inspiration, he pleased those disturbed by the incursions of contemporary science on traditional religious belief.

In serving the purposes of both blacks and whites, then, Carver's person was far more important than the substance of his work. If he would be sufficiently famous to serve those purposes, however, he must have major accomplishments beyond personal attributes alone. Thus, at the hands of the mythmakers—conscious or otherwise—he became the scientific wizard who saved the South.

Over the past two decades black scholars such as Herman R. Branson, E. Franklin Frazier, and Michael R. Winston have published books and articles containing informed assessments of Carver's scientific work. Most have compared it unfavorably with the important work of such unpublicized black contemporaries as Ernest Everett Just, a productive Howard University biologist, and Charles Henry Turner, an authority on insect behavior. Carver's much greater fame, they agree, derived from his folk appeal and his willingness to behave as whites wished blacks would behave. But the impact of these reassessments, limited in circulation, has been no match for the image perpetuated by the *Reader's Digest*, countless textbooks and juvenile biographies, the *Americana* and *Britannica* encyclopedias, the *New York Times*, and the Washington *Post*. Legends—especially useful ones—die hard.

Mr. Mackintosh is a historian with the National Park Service in Washington, D.C. *Much of the material in this article was first used by him in* The Journal of Southern History, *Vol. XLII, No. 4 (November, 1976).*

BROWN BROTHERS

WIDE WORLD

U.P.I.

U.P.I.

Carver the paragon (clockwise from top left): greeting Franklin D. Roosevelt during a presidential visit to Tuskegee, 1939; and with another celebrated admirer, Henry Ford, in 1942. The George Washington Carver Museum at Tuskegee was dedicated in 1941; the Liberty Ship S.S. George Washington Carver *was launched at Richmond, Virginia, two years later.*

IMAGES OF WAR

Jimmy Hare's Photojournalism

This photograph of an American battery was taken seventy-nine years ago during the climax of the Spanish-American War, at San Juan Hill in Cuba. "While the engagement was 'on,' " wrote the photographer, Jimmy Hare, of the day when Teddy Roosevelt made his famous charge, ". . . Stephen Crane and I struggled to the top of the ridge, where we met Richard Harding Davis. I think no other newspaper men were so far to the front as we." Up front was where Hare always wanted to be. Although today nothing like as well known as Crane and Davis, Hare in his prime was considered entirely fit company for them and by them; indeed, he was widely regarded as the top practitioner of what was then a new profession—photojournalism.

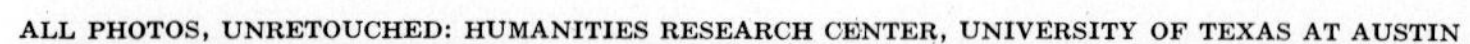

ALL PHOTOS, UNRETOUCHED: HUMANITIES RESEARCH CENTER, UNIVERSITY OF TEXAS AT AUSTIN

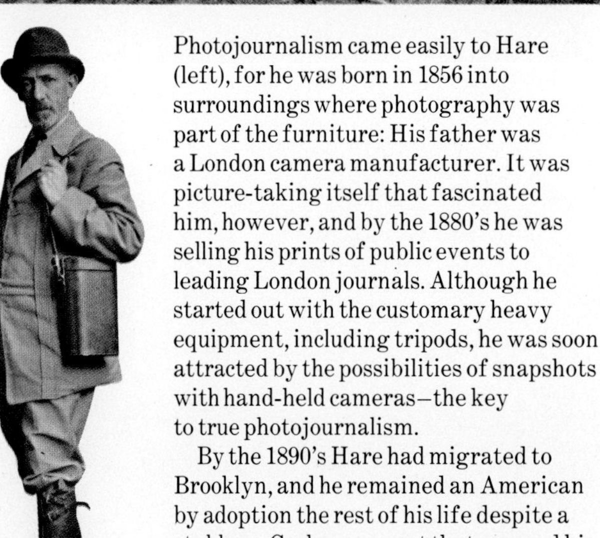

Photojournalism came easily to Hare (left), for he was born in 1856 into surroundings where photography was part of the furniture: His father was a London camera manufacturer. It was picture-taking itself that fascinated him, however, and by the 1880's he was selling his prints of public events to leading London journals. Although he started out with the customary heavy equipment, including tripods, he was soon attracted by the possibilities of snapshots with hand-held cameras—the key to true photojournalism.

By the 1890's Hare had migrated to Brooklyn, and he remained an American by adoption the rest of his life despite a stubborn Cockney accent that amused his colleagues. Between 1895 and 1898 he was a news-and-features photographer for *The Illustrated American*. When the battleship *Maine* blew up in Havana harbor early in 1898, Hare proposed to the editor of *Collier's Weekly* that he be sent to Cuba. That was the start of a series of war assignments that took him to Korea and China in 1904 for the fight between Japan and Russia, to Mexico in 1911 and 1914 to cover the revolution there, and "over there" for *Leslie's Weekly* between 1914 and 1918. He worked on after the war into the mid twenties, but gradually spent more and more time on the lecture circuit and with his grandchildren. He died in 1946 at eighty-nine, still revered as the grand old man of American photojournalism.

The Russo-Japanese War of 1904–1905 may be said to have been more pointless than most, since Russia courted it in the hope that it not only would keep Japan out of China and Korea, but would avert a revolution at home by inspiring the restless peasantry with patriotic fervor. Such hopes were severely dashed in a series of Japanese victories, and President Theodore Roosevelt was able to negotiate a peace in 1905. Meanwhile, the world's outstanding reporters journeyed to Japan to accompany the army to the field—among them Jimmy Hare. As it turned out, he seldom was allowed close to the action, but he still conveyed a vivid impression of the war in pictures like these: Japanese soldiers building a funeral pyre after a battle (opposite page); Chinese villagers anxiously awaiting Japanese occupation troops (above); Japanese soldiers improvising a bath at the front with the weather around zero (left).

The off-again-on-again character of the Mexican Revolution of 1911-17 made it hard to predict important events for news coverage, but Jimmy Hare nevertheless got into the thick of two of them—the siege of Juárez in 1911, and the American occupation of Veracruz in 1914. With the cooperation of the government garrison, he stayed in Juárez, across the Rio Grande from El Paso, during two days of fighting in May, 1911, often exposing himself to rebel fire in his effort to get good pictures. ("Do not take any more foolish chances," *Collier's* wired him upon hearing of this, to which the annoyed photographer replied: "Have evidently misunderstood my assignment. Will send you El Paso sky line and some pretty pictures of flowers in the park.") When the revolutionists took over the city, Hare was all set with his camera to catch the leaders as they rode into town to accept the surrender. His dramatic shot of Francisco Madero and his cavalcade—with his ally, Pancho Villa, at his left—was only moderately spoiled by Madero's choice of white shirt and tie rather than bandoleers as costume for the day. Above, right, Hare's portrait of a very young rebel sniper was more in keeping with popular expectations.

" 'Jimmy' Hare will cover the European War exclusively for *Leslie's*," that magazine announced proudly in August, 1914. By this time, however, nations and armies had learned the advantage of feeding a carefully censored version of war news to the public, and photographers were not wanted near the front. The famous photojournalist found himself restricted to rear areas, and even there had to submit all his photos for culling. In the face of these obstacles, Hare contrived to take a great many pictures that got past the censors and still projected some feeling of the horrors of World War I. When the *Lusitania* was sunk by a German submarine in May, 1915, he hurried to the Irish coast to record the shocked faces of survivors, the funeral procession, and (opposite page, above) caskets lined up for transportation. On an anticipated battlefield he snapped French soldiers working with one of the war's nastiest achievements, barbed wire entanglements; in Antwerp he clicked his shutter just as a German shell exploded down the street; in the same city he photographed citizens writing notices on the wall of a public building in an effort to find relatives lost during the bombardment.

These pictures are some of over a hundred selected for *Photojournalist: The Career of Jimmy Hare*, by Lewis L. Gould and Richard Greffe, just published by the University of Texas Press; our sketch of his life is also based on their text.—E.M.H.

ILLUSTRATED FOR AMERICAN HERITAGE BY MIKI

HOLLYWOOD'S GARDEN OF ALLAH

by George Oppenheimer

Tallulah Bankhead called it "the most gruesomely named hotel in the western hemisphere." Others, perhaps thinking of its curious architecture or the monumental hangovers that accompanied its boozy high life, called it simply the most gruesome hotel. To most of its denizens, however—to the scores of stars, writers, directors, wits, and wags who would stay nowhere else when they went to Los Angeles to "make a movie"—it symbolized Hollywood itself.

It is gone today, replaced, fittingly perhaps, by a many-storied bank. But from the late 1920's until the years immediately after World War II, the Garden of Allah on Hollywood's Sunset Strip was a hotel and an institution without peer. An uninitiated visitor might have passed it by without a glance. But rubbernecking tourists in buses that took them to see the homes of the stars were sure to have it pointed out to them. After gazing at the houses of the likes of Mary Pickford, John Gilbert, and Greta Garbo, they would roll past the restaurants and shops on the Strip, and then the guide with the megaphone would announce, "To your right, folks, the famous hotel, the Garden of Allah. Probably more luminaries living there right now than in all the rest of Hollywood put together." Through the window of the moving bus they got a fleeting glimpse of something sprawled out in a hollow below street level—red-tiled roofs smothered in tropical growth; a pink neon sign glaring in daylight among palm and pepper trees, sometimes with some of its letters failing to light up so that it announced THE DEN OF ALLAH.

"Garden" and "den" were equally appropriate. Some awed guests recalled the Garden as an earthly paradise. But Lucius Beebe, raconteur and expert on luxuriously riotous living, announced shortly after moving into the hotel that he had seen nothing like it for "concentrated alcoholism and general dementia" since the old days of the Harvard-Yale boat races during Prohibition.

The Garden in its prime (opposite), and Alla Nazimova, after whom it was misnamed

Generally, the hostelry lived up to its billing. The new arrival's neighbors often included stars such as Humphrey Bogart, Laurence Olivier, John Barrymore, Vivien Leigh, Gloria Swanson, Al Jolson, Clara Bow, W. C. Fields, and Errol Flynn, or perhaps such musicians as Igor Stravinsky, Leopold Stokowski, and Sergei Rachmaninoff, as well as swarms of celebrated writers, including William Faulkner, John Steinbeck, Ernest Hemingway, John O'Hara, F. Scott Fitzgerald, and Raymond Chandler.

The hotel began its life as a luxurious private home in 1920. Los Angeles County was then experiencing a mammoth real estate boom, and among the many speculators to profit from it was one W. H. Hay, who signalized his success by building himself a large house on Sunset Boulevard, surrounded by three and one half acres of formal gardens and framed by palms and other tropical trees. Under its tile roof were forty rooms, with floors of teak, and richly carved decorations in rosewood and pale mahogany. The mansion cost him some $200,000—considerably more than a million dollars in today's terms.

Hay enjoyed his munificent home for just four years, then leased it at $50,000 a year to Madame Alla Nazimova, a Crimea-

Clara Bow, the "It" Girl

born actress who was then one of the brightest stars of the silent screen. There was a blaze of publicity when she took possession of the place, and she spent a small fortune redecorating, adding new landscaping, and installing a free-form swimming pool whose shape, some claimed, had been inspired by the configuration of the Black Sea. When she was finished she modestly called the whole works the Garden of Alla.

Living there did not bring her much luck. Her picture career declined, she suffered personal as well as business troubles, and after two years of lavish entertaining, she had to turn over the lease to a corporation, which planned to convert the estate into a hotel. The house was remodeled to accommodate paying guests; many of the gardens were demolished; and single and duplex bungalows were built around the main building and the pool.

The grand opening of the new hotel on January 9, 1927, was in the gaudy tradition of the Hollywood première. Greeters in swallowtail coats and striped pants ushered thousands of unabashed gawkers through the rooms and bungalows, while a string quartet played in the lobby of the main building and a platoon of Japanese butlers served tea, punch, and sandwiches. When darkness fell, visitors gasped with wonder as colored lights lit up the grounds, and strolling troubadours in Spanish costumes sang and played beneath the night-blooming jasmine. The theatricality of the opening suggested the make-believe world of the movies, and it was assumed by most visitors—and reported by the newspapers the next day—that the new establishment would appeal most to movie makers.

They came in droves, and by the end of the first week the management knew that the Garden of Alla was a hit. Within a few months, common usage by the guests, and references by the Los Angeles newspapers, had permanently corrupted the spelling of the hotel's name; thereafter it became the Garden of Allah.

The Garden had opened at a turning point in Hollywood history; the Academy of Motion Picture Arts and Sciences had just been founded, and Al Jolson was at work on the Warner lot making the pioneer talking picture, *The Jazz Singer*. Jolson, an early Garden resident, typified the transplanted New Yorkers who first filled the hotel, setting an enduring tone that owed more to Broadway than to California and launching a home-away-from-home party that lasted more than twenty years. Once in a while during that time the hotel and cottages might have appeared somnolent; but the party smoldered on all the same.

"There were no rules," reminisced one early resident. "Nearly everybody drank, and drank hard. It was the thing to do, especially at the Garden. You would come back late at night and look around for a lighted window. That meant a party, where you'd be welcome." The informality took many forms. "If a stark naked lady of acting fame, her head crowned by a chattering monkey, chose to open the door to Western Union, no one was abashed, least of all the lady and the monkey," wrote Whitney Bolton, a New York drama critic who stayed at the Garden. But the informality was not for strangers and voyeurs. The hotel management posted a guard at the front gate and maintained a discreet patrol of the grounds after dark, one of the watchmen leading a formidable dog that residents fondly called the Hound of the Baskervilles. The private police were strictly for security; they had orders not to harass the guests or interfere with their personal foibles and pleasures.

Such guaranteed privacy soon produced a ceaseless stream of outrageous Hollywood stories. There was, for example, the tale of the Broadway playwright who was ensconced in a bungalow some distance from the main house. For weeks he had been trying to get into the office of an old acquaintance who was now the executive producer at a big studio. Day after day he had been turned away. Late one evening he heard a knock at his door and opened it. There stood the producer. "Hello, old boy," said the tycoon. "Come to my office tomorrow. I have a contract for you." The producer disappeared in the darkness, and next day the author signed his contract. Not till some time later did he learn that the producer had mistaken his bungalow for a similar one nearby in which he had recently installed a young lady.

Being on the Garden's guest list was a rough gauge of a film star's popularity. Clara Bow epitomized the flamboyance of the silent era at the Garden. Producers had advertised her to the world as the "It" Girl—"It" being sex appeal of overpowering voltage—and she was a popular figure at the poolside cocktail hour and at evening festivities as well. Occasionally diving off the high board in a dinner gown or pushing tuxedoed escorts into the pool, she made the evening-dress swimming party part of the Garden's early lore. But age overcame her and by 1937 her red Kissel roadster ceased to appear in its accustomed place in the parking lot, and her three chow dogs, whose coats matched their owner's hair, were no longer heard yapping at the bellboys. The "It" Girl was no longer a star.

By that time, Lucius Beebe had become one of the most active residents the place had ever seen. A columnist for the New York *Herald Tribune*, Beebe was an expert on railroading as well as good living, and had been engaged by director Cecil B. DeMille as technical adviser for the film *Union Pacific*. DeMille did not require Beebe's constant attendance at the studio, and so he had plenty of time to participate in—and lead—the life at the Garden. He would stand near the door of his bungalow as guests assembled and greet them with a cordial shout of "Welcome to Walden Pond." The Garden's room service especially impressed Beebe. The staff, he noted, could put a six-bartender private bar into operation on a minute's notice before lunch, so that those persons whom Beebe called "the maimed and dying from the previous night's party" could be given succor.

Not all the stories about the Garden were based on the Bacchanalia that went on there, though its reputation in that regard was so solidly recognized that H. B. Warner, who was about to play the role of Christ in a movie, was seriously warned by his director, C. B. DeMille, to remain in his bungalow and not get mixed up in the fleshpots of the hotel. Apart from the drinking, however, the resident wits gave the hostelry a general air of group merriment. Sheila Graham, from whose book *The Garden of Allah* many of these anecdotes come, termed it "the Algonquin Round Table gone West and childish." Musician Artie Shaw thought it "one of the few places so absurd that people could be themselves."

The Garden's easygoing management had a lot to do with the hotel's informal atmosphere. There was little pressure for prompt payment of bills, for example, even though some accounts carried charges for room service, gratuities to the staff, limousine hire, theater tickets, and cash advances in addition to rent. The owners had learned that in the long run they could depend on their tenants' high earning power.

One group of tenants, however, was denied credit. These were the Hallroom Boys, an assemblage of English actors who had flocked to Hollywood and who found occasional work as bit players in British Empire epics such as *The Lives of a Bengal Lancer*. These Englishmen, generally down-at-the-heels, inhabited the former servants' rooms in the hotel's main building. Their main occupation, it seemed, was to serve as stooges and jesters to the affluent residents of the bungalows. Wearing totally unwarranted Old Etonian ties, and blazers with the armorial emblems of Oxford and Cambridge colleges, with which they had no connection whatsoever, they amused their patrons with prattle about Sandhurst, the Guards, and tea on the vicarage lawn. According to John McClain, a New York drama critic and

Al Jolson, the Jazz Singer

F. Scott Fitzgerald, before the Crack-Up

frequent Garden guest, the Hallroom Boys lived on tequila and nibblings from the cocktail buffet. One day, as McClain was settling his weekly account at the desk, a Hallroomer interceded disapprovingly: "You mustn't do this, old man. Embarrassing for the chaps. If you do it again, your name will be posted for payment of bill."

Perhaps the most loved and lovable of all the Garden's residents was humorist Robert Benchley, who came to Hollywood to star in a series of shorts and shared one of the larger bungalows with his friend, John McClain. The Garden of Allah suited Benchley perfectly, and he became the genial familiar spirit of the place in the period of its final glory, which began as the 1940's came on. It was here that he is supposed to have said after leaving the pool that he believed he would get out of his wet clothes and "into a dry martini," a witticism as often repeated at the time as the cable he is supposed to have sent to David Niven from Venice: "Streets full of water. Please advise."

Stories of Benchley's association with the Garden are legion. Once he tried to phone New York at night but was unable to rouse the hotel operator. He finally went to the main house, upended some furniture, and left a note on the switchboard, reading, "Let this be a lesson to you. I might have been having a baby." On another occasion, he held forth at the pool to British novelist P. G. Wodehouse on the Hollywood "nodders." They were lower, he explained to the British author, than the studio "yes men," for after the "yes men" yessed a producer, he said, the "nodders" nodded. There was also a memorable night when Benchley was lured against his will into playing The Game, which he loathed, and was given to act out the name of Ladislas Bus Fekete, a Hungarian screenwriter who was then working at one of the studios. Benchley immediately dropped to his hands and knees and began to crawl around the room. Then, as his bewildered teammates tried to guess what he was trying to convey, he crawled across the floor and out through some French doors, disappearing into the darkness—to be seen no more that night.

One of the best-remembered Benchley anecdotes concerned a new doorman at the Garden. As Benchley brushed past him, the doorman stretched out his hand for a tip and asked, "Aren't you going to remember me, sir?" "Why, of course," Benchley replied. "I'll write you every day." Nevertheless, everyone at the Garden liked to be near Benchley, to hear his booming laugh and bask in his warm generosity. Sometimes his kindness got him into trouble. One evening in a bar on Sunset Strip, he encountered an odd little man, wearing a derby and pince-nez, who told Benchley he was a song writer and was working on a number entitled "Stars Fell on Orchi Chornya." Benchley was so tickled by this that he invited the man to drop in on him at the Garden any time he felt like it. Accepting on the spot, the song writer accompanied Benchley to the hotel and established himself in the spare bedroom of Benchley's bungalow. The visit was a disappointment to his host, for the man said nothing worth remembering, although he ate and drank heartily. After several days of free-loading, he put on his derby and left, remarking as he departed, "I'm sorry to have to eat and run."

Like many guests, Benchley was an out-of-place New Yorker, somewhat uneasy with the close-to-nature California life. He got along well enough with the Garden's cats and dogs, but waged a celebrated war against the large number of birds that flew around the grounds. One rainy Sunday, Benchley was peering out the living room window when McClain heard him explode with laughter. "You know the bird who keeps me awake all night," Benchley asked, "the one who sits outside my window and keeps saying, *'Chicago, Chicago'*?" McClain said he knew of this bird, and Benchley went on, "Well, he just came in through the rain for a landing. The tile around the pool was so wet his feet went right out from under him and he slid three or four yards on his tail, coming up against the edge of the pool. Then he looked over and saw me watching him, and I swear he shrugged his wings and his expression was, 'All right, you know me and I know you and this time *you* have the laugh.' "

Former residents all recall the contrast between the tranquil Garden and the frightful rush of traffic just outside. Benchley took careful account of this peril whenever he wished to visit The Players, a restaurant on the other side of the Strip. Instead of risking passage across the street on foot, he is reported to have turned right, walked one block to Schwab's drugstore, and jumped into a cab, which then made a U-turn and deposited him in front of The Players.

The increasing traffic Benchley so deftly avoided actually reflected the growth of Los Angeles into a great city in which moving pictures had become one of many major industries. Gradually, the movie people began to feel the loss of their unique importance and, along with the Second World War, there came a chill in the atmosphere of the Garden. Though the hotel had a short period of postwar prosperity, it was due more to the housing shortage than to the old magic of the place. In time, Hollywood notables stopped coming, transients from New York began to find lively new places to stay, and the Garden began to get the reputation of a beloved, but shabby, has-been. The hotel went through a series of management and ownership changes, and continued to deteriorate. By the late 1940's, even the once-dazzling landscaping had grown drab, for heavy smog, a new and baleful element in Los Angeles, had settled over the area. The Garden stood in a natural funnel for the noxious fumes that rolled up the Strip in such concentration that they split the tiles, asphyxiated the big brown rats in the palm trees, and killed the radiant bougainvillea.

Some of the new guests seemed equally obnoxious. The harmless Hallroom Boys disappeared along with the rich movie people, and the bar was often occupied by smalltime chiselers and petty racketeers. Drunken fights broke out, and the management often had to call the police—something unheard of in happier times. In its last years the Garden seemed like a setting from a story of the Los Angeles underworld by Raymond Chandler, himself long since moved away. One could imagine his private eye, Philip Marlowe, leaving his coupé in the Garden parking lot and meeting some dubious character in the bar. Things grew still worse: one night armed thugs entered the lobby, looted the cash drawer, and shot the elderly night clerk dead.

The last owners gave up in April, 1959, announcing that they had sold the property to the Lytton Savings and Loan Association; the Garden would be razed to make way for a banking and commercial center. The furnishings were sold at auction: comedian Ben Blue bought the china and silver for his nightclub. On the night of August 22, 1959, an attempt was made to hold a gala grand closing to mark the official passing of a place that had actually died some years before. Many guests dressed as old-time picture stars and tried to evoke a mood of civilized nostalgia, but on the whole it was an unfortunate affair. Only one genuine silent star stopped by—Francis X. Bushman, still a handsome, dapper man at seventy-six. He stood for a moment looking at the empty bottles floating in the pool, then shook his head, walked back to his car, and drove home.

George Oppenheimer, drama critic, screenwriter, playwright, and author of several books, was a frequent guest at the Garden of Allah.

For further reading: The Garden of Allah, *by Sheila Graham (Crown, 1970)*

Robert Benchley takes his ease at the Garden.

AN IMMODEST PROPOSAL: Nikita to Adlai

by John Bartlow Martin

In early January, 1960, Adlai E. Stevenson received a puzzling telephone call at his Chicago law office from Mikhail A. Menshikov, the Soviet ambassador to the United States. Stevenson, who had been the unsuccessful Democratic nominee for President in 1952 and 1956 and was still titular head of the Democratic party, had stated more than once—although some of his friends were not convinced—that he did not intend to run for the Presidency a third time, in 1960.

As John Bartlow Martin reports in the final volume of his biography of Stevenson, Adlai Stevenson and the World, *which Doubleday & Company will publish in October, Menshikov said that he had gifts and messages that Premier Khrushchev had sent to Stevenson via the embassy, and asked if he might come to Chicago to deliver them personally. Stevenson replied that* he *would instead call on the ambassador. The story of this peculiar, intriguing incident, which has never before been revealed, continues as told in Mr. Martin's forthcoming biography:*

On January 16, Stevenson was in Washington, and he paid his promised call on Ambassador Menshikov at the guarded, forbidding Soviet embassy. Stevenson and Menshikov had met several times before. The ambassador was an outgoing man, given to diplomatic courtesies as some Russian emissaries were not. The two men exchanged pleasantries; Menshikov offered caviar, fruit, other delicacies, and drinks. Then at last he came to the point. He carefully withdrew from his pocket a folded sheaf of notes written in ink on small sheets of paper and began to speak, obviously under tight instructions. Stevenson "hesitated for a week before making any record of this curious conversation," and then dictated the following memorandum:

"Before returning last week from Moscow, he [Menshikov] had spent considerable time alone with Premier Khrushchev. He [Khrushchev] wishes me [Menshikov] to convey the following: When you met in Moscow in August, 1958, he [Khrushchev] said to you that he had voted for you in his heart in 1956. He says now that he will vote for you in his heart again in 1960. We have made a beginning with President Eisenhower and Khrushchev's visit to America toward better relations, but it is only a beginning. We are concerned with the future, and that America has the right President. All countries are concerned with the American election. It is impossible for us not to be concerned about our future and the American Presidency which is so important to everybody everywhere.

"In Russia we know well Mr. Stevenson and his views regarding disarmament, nuclear testing, peaceful coexistence, and the conditions of a peaceful world. He has said many sober and correct things during his visit to Moscow and in his writings and speeches. When we compare all the possible candidates in the United States we feel that Mr. Stevenson is best for mutual understanding and progress toward peace. These are the views not only of myself—Khrushchev—but of the Presidium. We believe that Mr. Stevenson is more of a realist than others and is likely to understand Soviet anxieties and purposes. Friendly relations and cooperation between our countries are imperative for all. Sober realism and sensible talks are necessary to the settlement of international problems. Only on the basis of coexistence can we hope to *really* find proper solutions to our many problems.

"The Soviet Union wishes to develop relations with the United

In 1958, a friendly chat—this one face to face—was photographed by Stevenson's son, John Fell.

JOHN FELL STEVENSON, MAGNUM

States on a basis which will forever exclude the possibility of conflict. We believe our system is best and will prevail. You, Mr. Stevenson, think the same about yours. So we both say, let the competition proceed, but excluding any possibility of conflict.

"Because we know the ideas of Mr. Stevenson, we in our hearts all favor him. And you Ambassador Menshikov must ask him which way we could be of assistance to those forces in the United States which favor friendly relations. We don't know how we can help to make relations better and help those to succeed in political life who wish for better relations and more confidence. Could the Soviet press assist Mr. Stevenson's personal success? How? Should the press praise him, and, if so, for what? Should it criticize him, and, if so, for what? (We can always find many things to criticize Mr. Stevenson for because he has said many harsh and critical things about the Soviet Union and Communism!) Mr. Stevenson will know best what would help him.

"The presentation concluded with questions about 'Mr. Stevenson's rival,' meaning Vice President Nixon, and repeated declarations of desire not 'to interfere in an American election,' together with many sober statements about the profound 'interest' of the Soviet Union, and of all countries, in the American election. The protestations about non-interference were interspersed throughout the presentation, which I did not interrupt. The distaste and mistrust of Nixon was expressed cautiously but clearly. The Ambassador made a gesture of sad resignation about the Khrushchev-Nixon altercation in the model kitchen at the Trade Fair in Moscow, if not saying, at least implying, that Khrushchev had not realized that such an irrelevant dialogue recorded on television would be shown and taken seriously in the United States, to the great political advantage of Nixon.

"While it was not included in the formal presentation of Mr. Khrushchev's message, it was apparent that they were quite aware of the effect on the Presidential election of the [forthcoming] Summit Conference and Eisenhower's visit to Russia; that a 'success' would redound to the benefit of the Republican candidate which seems to leave them in some dilemma. [This summit conference, scheduled for the coming May in Paris, was cancelled by the Russians after they shot down an American U-2 spy plane over their territory.]

"Mr. Menshikov concluded by saying that this interview was the best evidence of the confidence reposed in me by the Premier and his colleagues and that he had no misgivings about my keeping it in confidence.

"At the conclusion, I made the following points:

(1) My thanks for this expression of Khrushchev's confidence.

(2) My thanks for this proffer of aid.

(3) However, I was not a candidate for the nomination and did not expect to be a candidate for the Presidency in 1960.

(4) My grave misgivings about the propriety or wisdom of any interference, direct or indirect, in the American election, and I mentioned to him the precedent of the British Ambassador and Grover Cleveland. (He in turn implied that President Eisenhower was not above intervention in the British election last fall; nor Dulles in behalf of Adenauer vs. the Social Democratic party in Germany.)

(5) Finally, I said to him that even if I was a candidate I could not accept the assistance proffered. I believe I made it clear to him that I considered the offer of such assistance highly improper, indiscreet and dangerous to all concerned.

"In thanking Khrushchev for his expressions of respect for my 'realism and understanding of the Soviet Union' I said that I hoped that I *did* have some understanding beyond the ordinary, and that I was sure Menshikov and Khrushchev had come to understand the U.S. much better, about which I found so much ignorance in the Soviet Union.

"I said that I was aware of some of the difficulties of the Soviet Union, especially with respect to China. At this point, Menshikov said with a wry smile: 'Yes, we may be allies again.'

"His manner was extremely amiable but very serious during his presentation of Khrushchev's message, which was done in a low voice, in a parlor adjoining the family dining room on the third floor. On two occasions when a waitress appeared with food, etc., he interrupted his conversation.

"On January 22, 1960, I wrote Mr. Menshikov the attached letter:

"'I am most grateful to you and Premier Khrushchev for the splendid gift you delivered to me at the Embassy in Washington last week. So much delicious Russian caviar and wine may not be good for me—but I like it! I hope you will extend my very warm thanks to Premier Khrushchev, and also my best wishes for his health and happiness in the New Year and the New Decade. That the year and decade will see ever closer and constantly improving relations between our great countries is my highest hope, and I am sure you and Mr. Khrushchev have similar sentiments about our common future.

"'The confidence expressed in me during our conversation and Premier Khrushchev's interest in my views were flattering and I wish I could thank him in person. But I must repeat that I will not seek the nomination for President again and that I do not expect to be a candidate of the Democratic party this year. Even if I was, however, I would have to decline to take advantage in any way of the confidence and good will I am happy to enjoy among your compatriots. I am sure you and Premier Khrushchev will understand, and I hope respect, my feelings about the proprieties in the circumstances we discussed, and I trust that my reaction will not be misconstrued as discourteous or ungrateful.

"'With renewed thanks to you and the Premier, together with my hope that we may have further talks from time to time, I am

Cordially yours,

[Adlai E. Stevenson]'"

Gathering up the dead
Common episode of the disaster
Scorched victims at Skunk Lake

THE HINCKLEY FIRE

by Richard F. Snow

ST. PAUL *Dispatch*, SEPTEMBER 3, 1894. MINNESOTA HISTORICAL SOCIETY, ST. PAUL

All through the late spring and summer of 1894 a haze of woodsmoke hung over the town of Hinckley in Pine County, Minnesota. Small fires burned unheeded in the cutover timberlands throughout the county, throughout the whole eastern part of the state. In mid-July, section gangs of the St. Paul & Duluth Railroad were out fighting fires north and south of Hinckley, and they succeeded in getting the flames under control before the right-of-way was damaged. At about the same time, a correspondent for a St. Paul newspaper observed: "The fires around here are spreading rapidly, and everything is as dry as tinder. Unless a heavy rain comes soon there may be a great loss sustained." Later, after the horror and the dying, those words would be remembered. But at the time all that the people in Hinckley and the nearby towns had on their minds was getting through the hottest, dryest summer any of them could remember.

This curiously negligent attitude toward the danger of fire had long been instilled in the settlers of the Pine County forests. For nearly a quarter of a century they had been clearing their farmlands by burning them over—a quick, easy, hazardous method. Drifting sparks would settle here and there, starting little fires that crept through the slash—debris left by the lumber operations—throughout the summer. Every once in a while a barn would go up, but prior to 1894 nothing really terrible had ever happened in Pine County.

Hinckley was a healthy, steady town of twelve hundred inhabitants, most of whom drew their livelihood in one way or another from the Brennan Mill Company, a big operation capable of cutting two hundred thousand board feet of lumber in a day. The town had an Odd Fellows' Hall, five hotels, eight stores, a restaurant, a town hall, three churches, eight saloons, a roundhouse, and two depots. The depots served two railroads whose tracks crossed just south of the town: the St. Paul & Duluth, and the Eastern Minnesota, which ran between Duluth and Minneapolis. This latter road had caused a good deal of annoyance to the citizens of Hinckley by digging an unsightly three-acre gravel pit right there in the town, and then refusing to fill it in. Now, in late August, the pit held about an acre of stagnant water.

At seven o'clock on the morning of Saturday, September 1, the Brennan Mill's whistle announced the beginning of another simmering, monotonous day. The smoke was thick enough to make the oxen cough in the outlying logging camps, but the Hinckley lumbermen were accustomed to smoke. The dust was worse; it had not rained for three months, and the haggard ground threw up white, choking clouds that made moving about a misery. The saws started up, and the ten-hour workday began.

Toward noon a stiff breeze blew up. The swamps west of Hinckley had been smouldering for most of the summer, and now the wind carried a gust of sparks from them into the mill yard. The piles of lumber stacked there began to burn. J. W. Stockholm, who worked in the Brennan company store, turned out with some others and hauled barrels of water to the yard. The wind died down and the men put out the fire, but Stockholm didn't like the look of things. He went to his home, and told his wife to "act quickly if it should come to look pretty bad, and have a few barrels of water ready . . . ." On his way back to the store, the wind came up again so strongly that Stockholm could scarcely keep his eyes open.

At about two o'clock John Craig, chief of the volunteer fire department, rang the gong that called the firemen to assemble at the engine house. "It looks threatening in the south and in the southwest," Craig told his men. "I don't think there is any danger, but it's well to be prepared for an emergency." Nobody thought there was much danger, even though the fires were burning again in the mill yard.

Craig's men ran out two thousand feet of hose, and soon had a

Top: James Root, who backed his train to safety. Above: Thomas Dunn, who died at the telegraph key.

TOP: *Memorial of the Minnesota Forest Fires*, BY WILLIAM WILKINSON, 1895. ABOVE: HINCKLEY FIRE MUSEUM, HINCKLEY, MINN.

job on their hands. The fires were growing, and threatening to cross the St. Paul & Duluth tracks into the town. The wind was rising, the smoke growing thicker. Men began to show up with wagons loaded with barrels of water.

Chief Craig ran to the St. Paul & Duluth depot and had Thomas Dunn, the telegrapher there, wire nearby Rush City for more hose. Craig returned to the fire, and Dunn's sounder started clicking. The last message he would ever receive told Dunn that Pokegama, a town nine miles to the south, was in flames.

At 2:45 P.M. Edward Barry, driving engine *No. 105* of the Eastern Minnesota Railroad, pulled into Hinckley with a freight drag. He found the town deserted—everyone was out fighting the fire, which was now coming on in a great, solid wall to the east, south, and west. The town wasn't burning, but the yards beyond the Eastern Minnesota depot were; the ties were on fire, and the rails warping. Barry ran his train onto a siding and sat waiting for the southbound passenger train, which was due in at 3:25.

To Barry's immense relief, it was running on time. Edward Best, the engineer on the passenger train, took his locomotive down to the water tank. The wind was blowing a full gale now, and burning embers showered George Ford, Best's fireman, as he struggled to take on water. The heat was terrific, and Ford was three times driven from the spout; but he knew that if the engine ran out of steam, crew and passengers would most likely die. At last the job was done, and Best spoke with H. D. Powers, his conductor. "What do you think of putting the freight engine behind us?" Powers asked. Best thought it a very good idea.

Powers was senior to the conductor on Barry's train, and so took command. He had Barry couple his locomotive to the rear of the train—the front, actually, since they would be backing up once they were under way—and got three empty boxcars hooked up.

Then the town of Hinckley virtually exploded. The very air seemed to be burning, and the roaring of the fire storm drowned out the screams of the townspeople. Dense smoke completely hid the sun, but as buildings took fire they briefly lit the howling darkness like flashes of lightning.

People began running for the train, and the crews helped them aboard. Best, at the front of the train, controlled the air brakes, which was fortunate, since Barry didn't want to wait. Barry gave two sharp tugs on the whistle cord—the signal to pull out—and began to back the train away from the depot. Before he got more than a few yards, however, Best jumped up into the cab of his own locomotive and put on the brakes. According to Best's fireman, Barry's conductor then came running over and shouted, "Barry will cut off his engine and pull out!"

"I guess not!" yelled Best.

It did, in fact, seem time to leave. The paint was melting and running off the cars, and the ties beneath them were afire. "It was at this juncture," said Best, "that excited men pushed women and children from the coaches in their mad haste to get in themselves."

Still, Best kept the brakes on. "I was constantly implored to go, but there was still time, and many lives to be saved by the waiting."

Up ahead, Barry's whistle kept screaming to start, and frame buildings half a block away were detonating like bundles of fireworks. Men, women, children, and animals fell burning in the street just yards away from the train. Finally, Best pulled the whistle cord and released the air brakes. The train backed out of the blazing town. It was already moving when J. W. Stockholm and his family scrambled into a boxcar.

Among those who were not aboard was Thomas Dunn, the St. Paul & Duluth telegrapher. The depot was burning above his head, and friends had begged him to save himself. But he was waiting for orders; the *No. 4* Limited was due on his line. So

HINCKLEY FIRE MUSEUM, HINCKLEY, MINN.

Memorial of the Minnesota Forest Fires, BY WILLIAM WILKINSON, 1895

Hinckley had as dedicated a crew of volunteer firemen (seen at the top) as any town could hope for, but when the fire came, it was more a matter of flight than fight. Scores of citizens escaped with the aid of James Root's locomotive (above). Five hundred more fled the holocaust on another train manned by engineer William Best (far left) and fireman George Ford (directly left).

BOTH: *Memorial of the Minnesota Forest Fires*, BY WILLIAM WILKINSON, 1895

Thomas Dunn stuck by his key while life, in the form of five scorched coaches and three boxcars, drew away from him.

In his cab, Best turned for a last look at Hinckley and saw houses "burning so rapidly that one could see bedroom sets and other contents of the rooms. The fire would seem to burn the sides right off the buildings, revealing the contents in the glare. Buildings seemed to melt rather than burn in the fierce glow."

Barry's tender had no backing light—not that one would have helped much—and so brakemen O. L. Beach and Peter McLaughlin climbed up on the car and, soaking each other with water, kept watch as the train backed up. It was a terrible job; burning embers kept swirling toward them through the scalding murk, and the forests were blazing all around. Just after crossing the bridge over the Grindstone River, a small, nearly dry creek north of Hinckley, Barry saw people running toward the train. He whistled twice as a signal to Best, and stopped. Some forty more refugees were pulled aboard. There were more coming, but the rails began to buckle with the heat, and there was no time to wait.

"Trees were thrown down," said Best, "and terror and death stalked through the forest and clearings. Our train seemed like a sentient thing, but how insignificant in that tempest of wind and flame."

But seven miles outside of Hinckley the air freshened a little, and two miles later the train entered the undamaged town of Sandstone.

Crew and passengers called to the people there to come aboard and save themselves. But despite the tall flames right outside town, and the obvious fate of Hinckley, not a single Sandstone citizen chose to leave. The train moved on, and an hour later Sandstone was gone and forty-five of its people dead.

Just beyond the town a bridge stood 150 feet above the Kettle River. As Barry approached it, he saw that it was afire from one bank to the other. That seemed to be the end of the Eastern Minnesota emergency train. But, incredibly, M.W.W. Jesmer and W. W. Damuth, the bridge watchmen, had stayed by their post. "For God's sake, go on!" Jesmer screamed to Barry through a storm of falling sparks. "You can cross it now and it will go down in five minutes." Barry ran the train across the trestle. He was no more than two thousand feet clear of it when the east end collapsed into the river.

Damuth, dazed, wandered toward the bridge and was killed. But Jesmer, his clothes on fire, climbed down into the river, where his wife and four children were waiting for him. Neighbors helped Jesmer keep his family above water. As he struggled against the current, Jesmer heard something howling. At first he thought it was Damuth, but as the flames died down he saw that it was his dog, stranded on the charred remnants of the bridge. For a day afterward the bridge was too hot to approach, but on Monday morning a railroad bridge builder scrambled up the supports with a rope and lowered the battered dog down to its master. The dog survived.

The train rattled on and at last reached Superior and safety. It had crossed nineteen bridges on the way, most of them burning. Both Best and Barry were blind when they got there, and did not regain their sight until the next morning. The two engineers and their crews had saved some five hundred lives.

Those were not the only lives the Eastern Minnesota saved that day, though the others were saved inadvertently.

When the blistering wind had risen to a point where it threw the water back in the firemen's faces, Chief Craig called a halt to the effort. He mounted his horse and rode through Hinckley shouting: "We can't save the town; it's burning at the south end; run to the gravel pit; don't lose a moment, but fly!"

More than a hundred people plunged into the fetid water of the railroad's eyesore, and all of them survived. Some cool citizens stood and directed them there. Bull Henly, the Hinckley section man, posted himself in the road near the gravel pit and forced fleeing townspeople into it. Father Lawler, a Roman Catholic priest who had made himself popular in the community by "minding his own business" and faithfully serving the volunteer fire department, called for people to go to the pit.

One panicked man called to the priest, "To hell with advice of that sort." He ran up the old post road toward Sandstone. It seemed a logical choice. The road led north, and the flames were lowest in that direction. Scores of people ran up that road, and 126 of them were caught in the swamp by a wave of fire. They died quickly. "When that wave struck them one wail of anguish went up from the whole people as one man, and in less than a minute after everything was still except for the roar of the wind and the crackling of the flames."

The man who heard that final cry was named Allen Fraser. He had been fleeing with his wife and two of his children up the fatal post road when his wagon took fire. He turned the team loose, pulled his family to the ground, and waited to die. Then he heard a noise, and looked up to see another wagon, driverless, coming through the smoke. He stopped the horses, saw that the wagon held four barrels of water, and lifted his family into them. The terrible wave of fire passed over. The horses died in their traces; the Frasers were unhurt.

Another crowd of panicked people was fleeing up the tracks of the St. Paul & Duluth. There were about two hundred of them, and they ran as fast as they could. The ties were burning under their feet, and every few yards a gout of flame would spurt from the woods and take one or two down. At last some thirty were dead on the tracks behind; the rest stumbled along as best they could. It seemed a hopeless race, until those in the front of the mob saw a headlight swinging toward them through the darkness.

Jim Root knew more about railroading than most people. He had been fourteen years old when he signed on with the Hudson River Railroad in 1857. He had driven General Sherman's wood-burning locomotives toward the sea during the Civil War and ran the first load of prisoners out of Andersonville. After the war he drifted west to visit an uncle in Minnesota, took a liking to the vicinity, and became an engineer on the St. Paul & Duluth.

By the time he took the *No. 4* Limited out of Duluth that awful Saturday, he'd been through twenty-four years of Minnesota railroading, and he wasn't much scared by smoke. "We have had to run through smoke time and time again every year," he said. "There have always been more or less forest fires in Minnesota."

Still, the run started out somewhat differently from most. The smoke was thick even in the Duluth depot, and not long after the train started south a porter had to pass through the cars lighting the overhead lamps.

As the train approached Hinckley the smoke lifted and the day brightened, but Frank Daugherty, who was traveling with his ten-year-old son Otto, was not reassured. "This lit up the atmosphere in a very peculiar way—into a sort of dull, glowing, yellowish twilight, which had a brilliant but at the same time unnatural effect on the things within the range of vision."

Root had pressed on diligently through "total darkness about forty miles" when he saw that lurid, beautiful light. In its glare he saw the desperate people running up the tracks.

He stopped the engine, climbed out and asked the first people who reached him—an old woman and her two daughters—what was going on. He could get nothing out of them but, "For God's sake, will you save us?"

He told them to get aboard the train, and then saw somebody he knew. It was Mr. Bartlett, who had run the railroad's eating house in Hinckley. "Everything is burned up!" screamed Bartlett.

The detritus of horror and a town reborn: at upper left, searchers dig out the bodies of an entire family, and at upper right another body is brought in from the woods. At middle left is the flooded gravel pit where many found salvation, and directly above is Skunk Lake, a shallow pond that sheltered others from the "tempest of wind and flame." At left is a rebuilt Hinckley, several months after the blaze; it rose from ashes and flourishes today—but it has never lost its memories of the fire.

LEFT: HINCKLEY FIRE MUSEUM, HINCKLEY, MINN.; ALL OTHERS: *Memorial of the Minnesota Forest Fires*, BY WILLIAM WILKINSON, 1895

Root waited while men with their eyebrows burned away threw their wives and children into the train. Earlier he had thought to make a run through the fire, but now he realized that this was bigger than anything he'd ever seen, and all he could do was back away from it. The flames were advancing around the train in great leaps; the treetops swayed in the gale and, swaying, tossed huge balls of fire through the forest to the tops of other trees.

Root had just started to back the train when something exploded nearby, and a shard of glass from the cab window sliced into his neck. At about the same time, he heard people yelling in the forest and looked to see three men making for the train. He stopped, and then realized that during the wait the fire might burn through the air hoses, thereby setting the brakes. So he started up again. Two of the men jumped onto the engine, the other fell behind. Root backed his train, the cut in his neck spraying blood on his overalls.

Back in the cars, Frank Daugherty felt himself fortunate; he had his son to care for, and hence was not frightened for his own life. The little boy was saying, "Have we got to die papa, have we got to die?"

Daugherty had just succeeded in convincing his son that everything was fine, when "a great big fellow, evidently a religious fanatic, with eyes bulging out of his head went through the car shouting, 'We are all going to heaven together.' "

The cars were burning and the window glass melting. John Blair, a sturdy black porter, passed up and down the aisles between the seats, reassuring everybody, talking calmly, and giving wet towels to women whose hair had caught fire. The towels were being handed out from the lavatory in the chair car. William Blades, a Duluth businessman, was soaking the towels when a panicked passenger caromed into him. "What chances do you think we have of getting out of this?" the man wanted to know.

"About one in twenty thousand," said Blades, and passed back another towel. There was nothing but yellow flame outside the coach windows.

Up in the cab, Root fainted and, falling on the controls, nearly shut off the steam. When he came to, the train was crawling up a slight grade with a scant ninety-five pounds of pressure showing on the gauge. Jack McGowan, the fireman, spilled some water on Root. "My God! Give me some more of that," said the engineer, who, revived, called for a bucket of water to dip his hands in. They were badly burned, and he didn't want to rub them together for fear the flesh would come off.

Dazed though he was, Root had long since given up any idea of outrunning the fire. He was making for Skunk Lake, a marsh with a small pond of scummy water. At last the engine rolled out onto the bridge above the marsh. Root stopped the train, and collapsed on the floor of the cab. McGowan tried to help him, but the engineer protested: "Leave me and go help the passengers into the water."

The fireman took a pail, and went out to join the conductor, who was dousing the burning steps so that people could get off.

The passengers tumbled into the lake while the fire boomed through the sky above them. When McGowan saw everyone was safe, he ran back and helped Root down into the water.

Root was a railroad man, and he had one job left to do. He had saved his passengers and his crew, but there was his train on the low bridge, the coaches all burning, and the engine threatened.

"You can't live on the engine for the coal is all on fire," McGowan told him when he heard what Root had in mind. But nonetheless McGowan went along when Root climbed back on the bridge, unhooked the locomotive from the burning tender, and drove it a little bit forward, away from the consuming blaze.

Root, McGowan, and the rest of the survivors huddled in the dank waters of Skunk Lake for four hours until the incandescent ground cooled, and then crept out. They sat shivering in the darkness, while near and far stumps and branches still burned fitfully. At length it was decided that three strong men would head south to seek help at Pine City, fifteen miles away.

The small party set off down the tracks, stepping over charred bodies as they went. They picked their way along until they reached Hinckley, where they saw nothing left standing save the roundhouse and water tower. Those two gaunt structures, the twisted railroad tracks, and level fields of rubble were all that remained to indicate that there had ever been a town there.

Men and women who had survived the fire in the gravel pit were prowling through the ashes. Peter Knudson, Hinckley's Presbyterian minister, had found a few watermelons, cooked in their skins, and passed these around. His wife milked a cow that had sought refuge in the pit, and gave the milk to the children.

The party from Skunk Lake, joined by a few of the gravel pit survivors, passed on through the ravaged town and found a handcar on the outskirts. They set off on this, and a few miles later came to a work train.

Once out, the news spread rapidly. On Sunday a relief train stocked with provisions set out from St. Paul. The next morning another train started out from Pine City. Aboard it were five thousand board feet of lumber and Frank G. Webber, who would be in charge of burying the dead.

Webber had a big job. The dead were everywhere. Many corpses were found in a running position, having fallen in mid-stride. One girl was found on her side with her hands clasped; she had apparently been praying when the flames took her.

That first morning, Webber and his men dug a trench sixty feet long, and in it placed ninety-six bodies, all burned beyond recognition. Drinking liquor to steady their nerves, Webber's men worked for three days, burying in all 233 corpses. Among them were the mummified remains of the 126 whom Fraser had heard die. Their clothes had been entirely burned away, and only the soles of their shoes remained.

The heat had been unbelievable. Barrels of nails had melted into one mass, and in the yards of the Eastern Minnesota, the wheels of the cars had fused with the rails.

On November 24, D. W. Cowan, the Pine County coroner, signed the official list of people who had died in Hinckley and in the nearby towns. There were 415 names on it.

And still the dead kept turning up. The fire had roared along for twenty miles, laying desolate tens of thousands of acres, and it was not until four years later, in May of 1898, that the last victim was discovered. The Hinckley fire had been a colossal disaster and, if not the most costly blaze in American history, it nonetheless had taken well over a hundred more lives than the notorious Chicago conflagration of 1871.

The town of Hinckley was rebuilt. Something of the spirit that helped rebuild it is evident in a small book about the disaster written a few months afterward by a man named Elton Brown. After more than two hundred pages of the most harrowing descriptions of the catastrophe, Brown concludes with the ingenuous note: "For particulars regarding lands and other data of interest to a person contemplating removal to the Northwest, application can be made to Mr. Wm. H. Phipps, Land Commissioner of the Northern Pacific Railroad Company . . . ."

Brown's book contains dozens of eyewitness accounts of the holocaust, but none sums it up so succinctly as that of C. P. Fadden, a railroad man on the St. Paul & Duluth who saw the town burn up. When asked to describe the experience, all Fadden had to say was that he "had been in hell, and saw everything there was to be seen except Satan himself." ☆

THE WAY I SEE IT **by Bruce Catton**

ETHICS & ARMAMENTS

DANIEL KRAMER

For an example of the way an incident of the distant past can put a revealing light on a problem of today, you might care to spend a moment considering the case of the Swamp Angel.

The Swamp Angel was a rifled cannon in a sandbag battery built in a South Carolina swamp in the summer of 1863 when the United States Army was trying to batter its way into Charleston. To enter Charleston from the sea, which was the only possible way to do it, the army must first destroy Fort Sumter at the entrance to the harbor. To destroy Fort Sumter, it developed, it would be necessary to mount numerous guns in the surrounding swamps to supplement the naval bombardment. After a great deal of labor the army managed to build a number of batteries; among them, the Swamp Angel.

This one was different. Instead of being designed to attack Fort Sumter, it was pointed off to the northwest, where the only possible target was Charleston, a little more than four miles away. The gun was an eight-inch Parrott rifle firing a 200-pound shell, but some special ammunition had been devised for this occasion—regular shell casings with a small bursting charge and a large quantity of the best substitute the Ordnance Department could invent for old-fashioned Greek fire. They were incendiary bombs, in other words, designed to shell a part of Charleston that contained numerous homes in which, to be sure, slept a great many women and children.

With everything in place, the Union authorities demanded that the Confederates immediately evacuate Fort Sumter and some supporting works on Morris Island. If the request was refused they would bombard the city.

According to the Unionists, the Confederates ignored the demand; according to the Confederates, the Unionists did not give them time to make an answer; and in any case, shortly after midnight on August 22, 1863, the bombardment began. That night the Swamp Angel dropped sixteen shells into Charleston. The next night it dropped twenty more. Then, unfortunately, the gun exploded and the party was over. It turned out, in addition, that the Greek fire that had been prepared just did not work very well, and no important conflagration was started.

A fizzle, not worth the money and labor it had cost. But the whole business is worth thinking about.

For sheer viciousness the basic idea of raining incendiary bombs on a sleeping city full of noncombatants was up to anything the twentieth century could think of. Americans in 1863 could not make incendiaries that would go off properly, and their ideas about long-range bombardment were hard to translate into action, but the will was there. Once the technical capacity was improved, the human race would lie at the mercy of its own darkest impulses, which go deep into primal pits somewhere beneath the Stone Age.

The thing that makes mankind so uneasy today is not the murderous quality of the weapons that lie to hand, but the notion that when you are at war absolutely anything goes. You hurt the other side in any way you can. So you live always on the edge of the abyss. You become infected by your own terror.

Americans did not invent all of this, of course. There is blame enough to go all the way around. But we do need to remember what the trouble really is. It will not do to blame the weapons. We are going to have to begin by blaming ourselves. Then maybe we can start applying a corrective.

JACK LONDON

The Man Who Invented Himself

by Andrew Sinclair

Jack London carved himself a special niche in the annals of American literature. Born in poverty in the first month of America's centennial year, he spent his boyhood suffering the rejection of an unloving mother and much of his young manhood as a careless delinquent, a waterfront roisterer, and a road bum, quite as mindless of his own self-destruction as any modern youth who wastes himself with drugs and hitchhikes the interstates from nowhere to nowhere else.

London pulled himself out of poverty and psychic and physical ruin by writing, and by the time of his death in 1916 was the highest-paid writer of his time. He also was the best-known American writer of his time, for he was, by his own creation, a public figure, a man who put more of his genius into his life than into his work, even though his output as a writer was prodigious. He constructed a myth of himself as a hero battling against the elements, against drink and death, a frail superman always locked in a struggle for survival and success.

He was the prototype of the writer who tries to live out his words to the full—but cannot, except in his writing. His politics were as radical as those of Upton Sinclair; his contempt for the gaseous certitudes of middle-class life as scathing as that of Sinclair Lewis; his flouting of convention in his personal life as startling as that of F. Scott Fitzgerald; his dedication to the masculine ethos as profound as that of Ernest Hemingway; and his instinct for the public eye as shrewd as that of Norman Mailer. He preceded and presaged them all, for in the process of inventing himself, Jack London invented the idea of the American writer as personality quite as much as artist.

The materials out of which Jack London constructed his life were rich—if largely tormenting. He was born out of wedlock in San Francisco on January 12, 1876. His dwarfish, spiritualist mother tried to kill herself when his vagrant, astrologer father deserted her. After Jack's birth, she married a Civil War veteran and widower, John London, so that her child could bear his name. The little boy was brought up with his two stepsisters like a tumbleweed, moving across the Bay to a succession of frame houses in the poor parts of the new town of Oakland. His mother never touched him with love, and terrified him, yelping at her seances with the voice of an Indian medium called Plume.

John London moved the family out to small farms off the Bay and then into the dry valleys of northern California, but his wife's schemes for getting rich quickly ruined his agricultural ventures. The boy began to have the nightmares that disturbed his short sleep all his life, as well as the dreams of escaping his pinchpenny world for one of glittering and lavish fantasy. Thrown back into the slums of Oakland, Jack became a delinquent, a rebel with a cause. He wanted to leave his loveless mother, and he bought a skiff to sail the Bay toward the Golden Gate, challenging the rollers made by the side-wheel steamers, beating against the wind to Goat Island, yearning after the clippers that tacked toward the west and the other side of the world. The moment he could leave school, he joined the waterfront gangs, becoming an oyster pirate and a young drunk and a road kid, riding the freights up to the Sierras. He seemed reckless of his life, wasteful of his strong body, his small hands battered from fights.

He might have died young like most of the other victims of the raw port of Oakland, if he had not been bookish and determined. He had always loved reading—his mother had slipped down the social scale from an educated family. To him, the shortest ways out of the slums were the pages of Ouida or Washington Irving or Prescott. He also had the gift of organizing himself—so much time for earning money, so much time for reading, so much time for play. He knew that there must be a better world for him than the dockside saloons or the scrounging gentility of his mother's pretensions. Also his occasional months of dulling toil in a cannery or a jute factory gave him the resolve never to become an industrial slave.

PRECEDING PAGE: *Detail from a poster advertising a lecture on socialism by London, 1906*

JACK LONDON HISTORIC STATE PARK, GLEN ELLEN, CALIF.

So, in 1893, at the age of seventeen, Jack signed on as a sailor on a three-masted schooner, bound for the Bering Sea on a sealing expedition. He learned his new life quickly, even taking the wheel in a storm on one occasion. It was his first moment of mastery, of power and conquest. "In my grasp the wildly careering schooner and the lives of twenty-two men," he wrote many years later. "With my own hands I had done my trick at the wheel and guided a hundred tons of wood and iron through a few million tons of wind and waves. . . . When I have done some such thing, I am exalted." It revealed to him his pride in being a man who could pit his own small self against the worst that nature could do to him.

The voyage also taught him about the bloody business of life. There was month after month of following the seal herd, killing and stripping the skins off the pretty beasts, then flinging their carcasses to the sharks that followed the boat for their share of the massacre. This daily slaughterhouse was the young sailor's first sight of nature red in tooth and claw. The men were more bestial than the animals they killed. It was a crude, commercial competition, dictated by the market in furs. Jack began to see that the struggle among humans to live was part of the battle among species to survive. The men got the wages, the captain took the profits, the women wore the furs, the sharks devoured the meat, the masses of the seals died.

Yet the sea was only a place to escape to, not to work upon. He returned to factory jobs and heaving coal in Oakland in a time of national depression. When his free spirit could endure no more, he took to the road. Although he went with "Kelly's Army," California's detachment of Coxey's army of the unemployed, which set out for Washington, D.C., in 1894, he was no radical when he started, just a young man on the loose. In fact, he rode a raft down the Mississippi like Huckleberry Finn, eating the food he was supposed to be begging for the mass of the marchers behind, and he deserted the army at Mark Twain's home town of Hannibal. As he wrote later in *The Road*, he went on the bum because he could not keep away from it; he did not have the price of the fare in his jeans; he was so made that he could not work always on the same shift; and, finally, "just because it was easier to than not to."

So Jack turned into a thoughtless road kid, until a month in Pennsylvania's Erie County Penitentiary on a charge of vagrancy made a radical out of him. Jack saw in the jail the depths of human degradation, a society of degenerates and misfits tyrannized by a few trusties and hallmen, who shamefully exploited their fellow prisoners. To him, it seemed a parable of the whole of industrial America. He found himself living one of his childhood nightmares about falling into the stench and darkness of a bottomless pit. The alternative was the tooth-and-claw fight for social success, and upon his release he returned to his mother's home in Oakland, determined to educate himself.

Then began a frantic pursuit of knowledge. Jack was brave to go to high school after dropping out of the educational system for six years. His schoolmates were so young that he felt he was in a kindergarten. To them, he was an object of fear, an unbelievably shabby and careless man who had been a tramp and who chewed tobacco. His determination was so great, however, that after only two years he qualified in 1896 as a special student to enter the University of California at Berkeley.

Yet already a pattern in his career had begun to emerge. The rootlessness of his upbringing made him stick at no job or plan of study for too long. He had been brought up on the move, and he remained on the move in restless California. Whenever the pressures on his life seemed too great for him, he would pack up and go. Early in 1897 he dropped out to become a writer, because gossip about his birth was too much to bear; what was more, by then Jack had learned of and had contacted his real father—who had promptly denied his paternity. Jack was now determined to succeed on his own, without the help of the society that had made him poor, of the mother who did not love him, of the father who had deserted and denied him. Isolated, he determined to be utterly self-made—and how better to do it than by writing?

He worked at this new trade as diligently as ever, but found only frustration. The one anchor in his drifting, driven young life was his socialism, to which he had been converted by his jail, road, and sea experiences and by the books he read so voraciously. Radical socialism, he was now convinced, was the only thing that could keep men from being degraded and thrown out of work and crippled by the factory system. At the same time, the horror of the vicious struggle to survive in the gutters of America had hardened Jack's dreams into a fierce personal ambition. "I had been in the cellar of society," he later wrote, "and I did not like the place as a habitation. . . . If I could not live on the parlor floor of society, I could, at any rate, have a try at the attic. It was true, the diet there was slim, but the air at least was pure."

Although Jack's socialism was the passion of his life and made him many friends among the young radicals of San Francisco Bay, he did not put the good of the cause before his ambition for himself. He left California to look for instant fame and fortune in the Yukon gold rush of 1897. It was a stampede to illusion. He started off with enormous enthusiasm and energy, backpacking up Chilkoot Pass and getting to Dawson City before the ice froze the river. He staked a claim, but when he saw the actual grim drudgery of extracting a few ounces of gold from tons of frozen gravel, he did not stay to work it. The fact that he caught scurvy and hated to be ill also sent him back home to cure himself. The trip back to the sea two thousand miles down the river inspired him to keep a detailed diary. There was a gold mine, perhaps, in writing about Alaska.

Such was Jack's energy, such was his presence and power, that he convinced everyone he met that he would finally succeed in spite of his chopping and changing his goals. The descriptions of him as a young man were lyrical about his potential. "He had a curly mop of hair which seemed spun of its gold"; one of his friends wrote, "his strong neck, with a loose, low, soft shirt, was bronzed with it; and his eyes were like a sunlit sea. His clothes were flappy and careless; the forecastle had left a suspicion of a roll in his broad shoulders; he was a strange combination of Scandinavian sailor and Greek god."

One of his great loves, Anna Strunsky, was even more struck by his charisma, when she first met him at a socialist conference in San Francisco. She felt a wonderful happiness, as if she were meeting Lord Byron or Karl Marx in their youth. She was certain that Jack would become a character known in history. She saw a "face illumined by large, blue eyes fringed with dark lashes, and a beautiful mouth which, opening in its ready laugh, revealed an absence of front teeth, adding to the boyishness of his appearance. The brow, the nose, the contour of the cheeks, the massive throat, were Greek. His form gave an impression of grace and athletic strength. . . ."

Such was the force of Jack's presence, when he had achieved nothing. He could get what he wanted from people by awing them with his energy and conviction. He could persuade them of anything that he passionately believed about his future. Now he had to get what he wanted from his prose, for he had decided that writing short stories for the magazines offered the quickest rewards and the shortest route to fame. He modeled his style chiefly on Rudyard Kipling. Kipling had offered the world his myth of India and the mission of the British Empire. Jack would offer the world his myth of Alaska and the struggle of the fittest to survive in the northern wilderness.

Jack imitated his master well, but his Alaskan short stories possessed a raw force, a sense of elemental struggle, that Kipling never achieved. By 1903 the young Californian writer was a national name; three years later, he was known throughout the world. By 1906, before he was thirty years old, he had already written eight books, among them his two classics, *The Call of the Wild* and *The Sea-Wolf*. Yet the incredible swiftness of his success led him to form a reverse myth about it—that he had been forced to fight every inch of the way against every possible obstacle to reach what all young writers dream of and few attain.

It was true that Jack had written night and day for some years. Yet when the break arrived, it came with the suddenness of the white-water rapids he had ridden in Alaska.

In 1900, not long after their magazine publication, his early Alaskan stories had been issued in book form as *The Son of the Wolf*, which had been instantly acclaimed. Two other collections had swiftly followed. But when he became successful, Jack chose to speak of his hard head, hard work, and will power, not of his genius or his good fortune. He forever after insisted that the young author should write all the time and for a market. Once an author had a name, he could sell anything he wrote—good, bad, or mediocre. That was certainly true in Jack's own case. Yet his insistence that genius meant little, while sweat and salesmanship meant much, belittled his own powers. "Don't loaf and invite inspiration," he advised one colleague. "Light out after it with a club." He did harm to his reputation by denying his own special gifts as a writer. He claimed that he was a realist who wrote straight from the shoulder. In fact, he was a mythmaker who disturbed the reader with the depths and shadows of his prose.

His determination to show his own life and his writing as a struggle for survival he justified by his belief in a combination of social Darwinism and Marxist dialectics. To him, evolution was the first faith, revolution the second faith. Mankind evolved by the struggle against nature, society evolved by the war of the classes. He himself had developed by his determined revolt from the slums and manual labor of his background. His own efforts had made him an educated man and a famous writer. He would now impose his vision on his readers, and he would redeem a youth of failure by a manhood of success.

His first goal was to reach the parlor floor of society. Already, in 1900, he had married a strong, practical, educated woman called Bess Maddern, so that she could look after his home and raise his children. It was a marriage of convenience for a young writer making his way, and he defended his cool choice with logic. Unfortunately, he soon felt confined by domesticity, and he began a passionate affair with Anna Strunsky, the beautiful radical heroine of the Bay Area socialists. He even collaborated with her in writing a book, *The Kempton-Wace Letters*, published in 1903; in it, as "Herbert Wace," he hopelessly defended his calculated marriage against the romantic criticisms of Anna, as "Dane Kempton." Much as he loved his two young daughters and his planned life, he could not suppress his feelings or his ferocity, and once again he translated frustration into movement.

He was offered a job reporting on the aftermath of the Boer War, but when he reached Britain, the job was cancelled. He stayed in London to watch the coronation of King Edward VII, then he disappeared into the slums of the East End to research and write his passionate outcry against the degradation of the London poor, *The People of the Abyss*, also published in 1903. While

CONTINUED ON PAGE 106

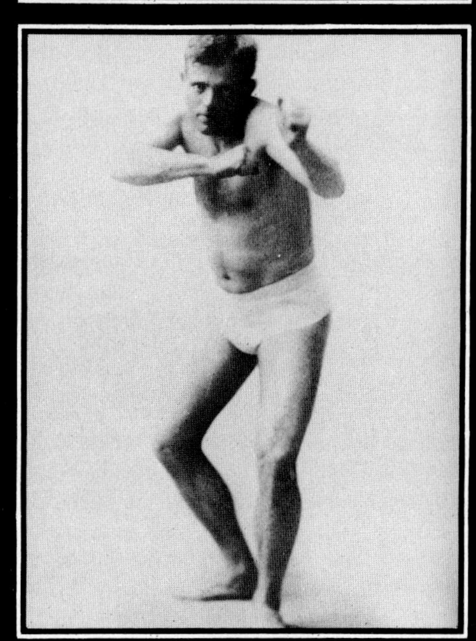

Top: Jack with childhood friend, Mable Applegarth; he is the one at the right. Bottom: as an amateur but belligerent pugilist, 1905.

Top: two portraits, ca. 1902—at the left as the roughhouse adventurer, at the right as the sophisticated young author.

Directly above: footloose as always, London joined "Kelly's Army" for a march on Washington, D.C., in 1894. He abandoned the crusade halfway there, but is seen at ease and grinning in the bottom right corner.

LONDON ON LONDON...

Only a man who has undergone famine can properly value food; only sailors and desert-dwellers know the meaning of fresh water. And only a child, with a child's imagination, can come to know the meaning of things it has been long denied. I early discovered that the only things I could have were those I got for myself.

—*John Barleycorn*, 1913

Perhaps the greatest charm of tramp-life is the absence of monotony. In Hobo Land the face of life is protean ... where the impossible happens and the unexpected jumps out of the bushes at every turn.... The hobo never knows what is going to happen the next moment; hence, he lives only in the present moment....

—*The Road*, 1905

Martin had enjoyed the fight, with a recrudescence of the old fighting thrills. But they quickly died away, and he was oppressed by a great sadness. He felt very old—centuries older than those careless, care-free young companions of his other days. He had traveled too far to go back.... He was too far removed. Too many thousands of opened books yawned between them and him.

—*Martin Eden*, 1909

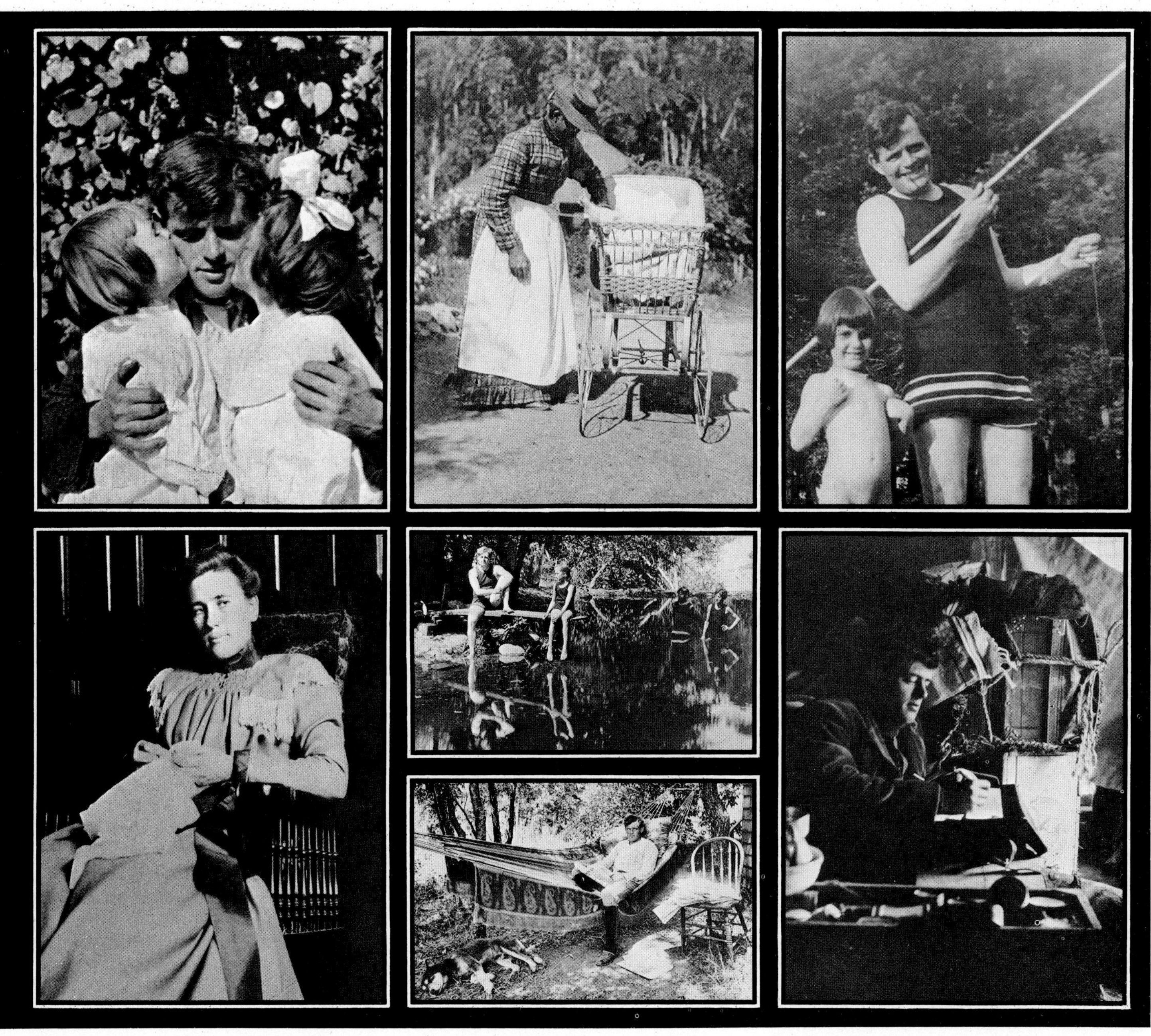

Top: with his daughters, Becky (right cheek) and Joan (left cheek). Bottom: London's first wife, Bess, about 1902.

Varieties of domestic bliss: at the top, Jack's photograph of daughter Joan with her "Mammy"; in the middle, he relaxes at a swimming hole with friends; at the bottom, in hammock in a bosky dell.

Top: cavorting with a neighbor's uninhibited child. Bottom: at work during the Russo-Japanese War, 1904.

Civilization has spread a veneer over the soft shelled animal known as man. It is a very thin veneer. . . . Starve him, let him miss six meals, and see gape through the veneer the hungry maw of the animal beneath. Get between him and the female of his kind upon whom his mating instinct is bent, and see his eyes blaze like an angry cat's, hear in his throat the scream of wild stallions. . . . Touch his silly vanity, which he exults into high-sounding pride, call him a liar, and behold the red animal in him that makes a hand clutching that is quick like the tensing of a tiger's claw, or an eagle's talon, incarnate with desire to rip and destroy. —*The Call of the Wild*, 1903

Marriage means less to man than to woman? Yes, by all means, at least to the normal man or woman. As surely as reproduction is woman's peculiar function, and nutrition man's, so surely does marriage sum up more to woman than to man. It becomes the whole life of the woman, while to the man it is rather an episode, rather a mere side to his many-sided life. Natural selection has made it so.

—*The Kempton-Wace Letters*, 1903

Top left and lower middle: Anna Strunsky, the darling of Bay Area socialists and for a time the mistress of London's heart

Top: after his affair with Anna Strunsky, London vowed that love would never again warp his life; but then came Charmian, his "Mate-Woman" and second wife. They are seen together here about 1905.

Directly above: London flaunts his machismo *with poet George Sterling, his close friend and the informal leader of the Bay Area's gaggle of literati.*

LONDON ON LONDON...

Heavens, how I wrote! Never was there a creative fever such as mine from which the patient escaped fatal results. The way I worked was enough to soften my brain and send me to a madhouse. I wrote, I wrote everything.... On occasion, I composed steadily, day after day, for fifteen hours a day. —"Jack London by Himself," in *Mainly About People*, 1910

The man's stooped and narrow shoulders and weazened chest proclaimed him the true child of the crowded ghetto.... To Martin, this withered wisp of a creature was a symbol. He was the figure that stood forth representative of the whole miserable mass of weaklings and inefficients who perished according to biological law on the ragged confines of life. They were the unfit. —*Martin Eden*

No, I am not in love. I am very thankful that I am not. I pride myself on the fact. As you say, I may not be adjusting my life artistically to its environment... but I do know that I am adjusting it scientifically. I am arranging my life so that I may get the most out of it, while the one thing to disorder it, worse than flood and fire and the public enemy, is love.
—*The Kempton-Wace Letters*

Top: bringing home a feathered prize at the Beauty Ranch near Glen Ellen. Bottom: scribbling away at a summer retreat called Wake Robin in 1904.

In the last months of his life, bloated and in almost constant pain, London nevertheless struggled to maintain his image. At the top, he is seen in his ranch house study; in the middle, on board the sloop Roamer; *at the bottom, with Charmian.*

Directly above: in one of the last photographs of him ever made, London takes the helm of the Roamer, *1915; he is thirty-nine years old.*

Martin questioned the validity of his popularity. It was the bourgeoisie that bought his books and . . . it was not clear to him how it could possibly appreciate or comprehend what he had written. His . . . beauty and power meant nothing to the hundreds of thousands who were acclaiming him and buying his books. He was the fad of the hour . . . who had stormed Parnassus while the gods nodded.

—*Martin Eden*

The dice were loaded. Those that died did not win, and all died. Who won? Not even Life, the stool-pigeon, the arch-crapper for the game—Life the ever-flourishing graveyard, the everlasting funeral procession. —*Burning Daylight*, 1910

. . . it is a terrible ordeal for a man to stand upright on his two legs unswaying, and decide that in all the universe he finds for himself but one freedom, namely, the anticipating of the day of his death.

—*John Barleycorn*

CONTINUED FROM PAGE 101

he was away, Anna Strunsky came to her senses and ended their affair. She would not risk a scandal by carrying on with a married man. Jack was bitter, but he had to accept the blow, stating that in the future he would confine romance to the pages of his books.

Yet he still chafed at domesticity, and his next two great books mirrored his mood—what he called his "long sickness." *The Call of the Wild*, his third published book in 1903, was about a dog that reverted to savagery in the wilderness; but it was also about Jack's own demand to be free. Thereafter, he called himself Wolf to his friends and he identified his nature with that lone animal's. *The Sea-Wolf*, published in 1904, told of the fight to the death between an educated sissy, Humphrey van Weyden, and a blond beast, Captain Wolf Larsen, on his sealing schooner. The characters may have represented Jack's own divided nature, with his willed concentration on self-education and the discipline of writing at war with his passion to be a physical superman.

Actually, his body had already begun to crack up on him when he lamed himself permanently on a voyage to Korea, where he reported the Russo-Japanese War in 1904. There he began riding horses the way most sailors do, lurching in the saddle as if on the deck of his sloop. He never walked a long way again, although his Alaskan heroes like Smoke Bellew were capable of vast journeys on foot. In Korea, however, he displayed both his boldness and his new taste for authority, sending back the first photographs of the Japanese Army in action and engaging the first of his two Oriental body servants, who would travel with him and look after him all the rest of his life.

Waiting for his return from Korea was Charmian Kittredge, his new mistress. She was one of the rare liberated and independent women of California, a good sportswoman and stenographer, five years older than Jack, with a trim figure. She flung herself into the affair with Jack, and she joined him in the horseplay and practical jokes that he loved. There was a fight for Jack's possession between her and "The Crowd," the group of radical artists and writers led by Jack's great friend, the poet George Sterling. Charmian won and persuaded Jack to leave his wife and family for a little ranch up in the Sonoma hills near Glen Ellen. The only way to cure his "long sickness" of restlessness and divided loyalties and appetites, she argued, was to put down an anchor with her on a piece of land. He accepted the solution, divorced his wife, and married Charmian. Where his stepfather had failed on the land, Jack decided, he would succeed. Where his first marriage had foundered in domesticity, his second would work with Charmian as his true love and "Mate."

So began the happiest period of Jack's life, the years 1905 and 1906, when he indulged all his contradictory urges almost simultaneously. When the Russian Revolution broke out, he toured the United States, giving a lecture on "Revolution" even at Yale and Harvard. He became the leading orator of the radical movement at the same time that he was setting himself up as a California rancher and writing imperialist articles for the Hearst press. He believed both in the superiority of the white man and in the eventual victory of the proletariat—but it had to be the white proletariat that won. Yet when he came to write his chilling prophesy of the "inevitable" world revolution, *The Iron Heel*, published five years later, in 1910, he foresaw the triumph of Fascism before the brotherhood of the workers could eventually rule the earth. And then—typically—at the height of his commitment to the Red cause and the California earth, he suddenly announced that he would set off in 1907 on a seven years' cruise around the world in a sailing boat, which cost him $30,000 to build and was rightly called the *Snark*, being a splendid illusion.

Such a series of contradictory actions in so short a space of time was remarkable in a man who insisted that he was rational, candid, and uncomplicated. In fact, he imposed a structure of apparent logic on violent and uncontrolled appetites, which had been deprived and now were indulged. He believed that he had been fed too little meat when he was a boy. Now he ate "cannibal sandwiches" of bleeding beef on the waterfront and almost raw duck twice a day in season, even if this did give him dysentery. He had been short of money all his childhood. Now he would take any hack-writing job that paid well, only to waste the money, as though he needed the whip of debt to keep him writing his thousand words a day.

His toil had to be voluntary. If he had suffered as a work beast under the factory system in the past, he would now preach a cause that asked the workers to take over the factories from their exploiters. If he had often fought and lost against other boys, now he would only play at fighting with his guests and report prize fights for the Hearst papers. If his mother and father had rejected him, he would proclaim to the world that he was utterly self-made and owed nothing to anyone. He would be loyal to those who were loyal to him, his stepsister Eliza, and his second wife Charmian; but when his mother and his wet nurse took the side of his first wife and his children after the divorce, he cut the two of them out of his will and most of his life.

He had made his way against everyone and everything. Defiantly he proclaimed that he would do what he wanted. "The ultimate word is I LIKE," he declared in the foreword to his account of *The Cruise of the Snark*, published in 1909. "It lies beneath philosophy, and is twined about the heart of life.... It is I LIKE that makes the drunkard drink and the martyr wear a hair shirt; that makes one man a reveler and another man an anchorite; that makes one man pursue fame, another gold, another love, and another God. Philosophy is very often a man's way of explaining his own I LIKE."

Yet what if a man wanted drink and revolution, revelry and intense study, fame, gold, love, and faith in mankind all at once, as Jack did? He could only try to do everything simultaneously, at the waste of his energy, at the eventual cost of his life.

If that extraordinary energy, that superb body and willpower had remained as strong as they had been most of his life, Jack might have achieved many more marvels, and he certainly would have damned their contradictions. But his sea voyage began the rapid deterioration of his body. After two years of wandering about Polynesia, he was suffering from five diseases. The worst of these were pellagra and yaws. Unfortunately, no cure was known for pellagra at the time, while yaws was treated like a form of syphilis by arsenic compounds.

As a man who declared that he was self-made, he believed in self-help. Aboard the *Snark*, he was both doctor and dentist. He had a large wooden medicine chest stuffed with bottles of drugs. He believed in dosing himself and his wife and his companions. He did not believe in tolerating physical pain that could be eased. Like many a Californian, he believed that the birthright of the western child was a promise to live forever. It was intolerable that the body should go wrong.

Yet his body did go wrong rapidly after 1908. The steady drinking that Jack described in *John Barleycorn* (1913) attacked his liver. Yet that was nothing to the remedies he injected into himself to cure his imagined diseases. Jack consequently thought that there was still a lingering taint of yaws in him. So he took a course of the new miracle remedy, salvarsan, invented in 1909. It had an arsenic base and had not been properly tested. The result was that Jack, while trying to cure himself of a disease that may have already passed through his system, was killing himself with a remedy that was a poison. The arsenic in the salvarsan attacked his nerves, his kidneys, and his bladder.

The deterioration in Jack's physique and stability has been

falsely attributed to many causes, chiefly psychiatric. In fact, the chief cause was bad medication. His kidneys and bladder were being steadily destroyed, until he could hardly sleep or concentrate, although he still managed to keep up a heroic schedule of work. He was a dying man, but he refused to admit it. Unfortunately, as the pain grew more intolerable, so grew Jack's reliance on sedatives such as alcohol and morphine. He had to dull the pain. His pride and his sense of his body's worth would not allow him to show weakness. In a way, he became the victim of his own myth of himself as a man who could endure all.

Ironically, his last years on his Beauty Ranch at Glen Ellen began to resolve the contradictions in the man. He started to come to terms with the legend that he had created. Fiction and person approached each other. He learned to accept himself and to postpone some of his desires. He remained loyal to Charmian, if not always faithful to her. He devoted himself to the development of the ranch. Where the soil was looted, he enriched it. Where weeds grew, he put in crops and vines and eucalyptus. He bred prize pigs and cows and Shire horses. He wanted to redeem the failure of his stepfather on his small ranch by making a success of large-scale farming. He countered the instability of his nerves with plans for the land that stretched over decades. Instead of a Red revolution in the cities, he now preached a green one in the countryside. He no longer echoed Marx, he prophesied Mao.

The novels of Jack's later period were less successful, because he was giving up the pretense of himself as an Alaskan superman for a version of himself as the new California rancher. Yet one of them, *The Valley of the Moon*, published in 1913, was as poignant and modern as today's dream of organic living. Jack took as his heroes a young worker and his wife, Billy and Saxon Roberts, who are broken in the labor battles of Oakland and take to the road. They go on a pilgrimage through rural California with tent and Hawaiian ukelele, seeking a patch of ground to farm and to set themselves up in life. It is a romance of young love and nostalgia for the soil, with a sweetness not to be found in the rest of Jack's writing—his admission that, when he was not racked with pain, he had found himself in his life with Charmian on the ranch.

He could not, however, completely escape his contradictory nature. His desire to settle on and develop the ranch was in conflict with his urge to run away from such responsibility. In his last years, when he called himself only a scientific rancher, he drove a four-in-hand through northern California, lived for months on end on his sloop *Roamer*, sailed round the Horn on a clipper, went to Veracruz to report on American intervention in the Mexican Revolution, and spent two long vacations in Hawaii, where he could hide his sickness and lethargy under the easy demands of the social life there. His last service to the legend of himself as a physical hero was his promotion of surfing, which he helped popularize as the supreme California sport.

Yet even he knew that he could not keep up the fiction of himself as a superman. The two autobiographical books of the last decade of his life demonstrated his increasing awareness of himself as a tormented man rather than a legendary pioneer. Although *Martin Eden*, published in 1909, overdramatizes his struggle to literary fame and fortune, it faithfully records his turning away from middle-class values and bookish success. *John Barleycorn* is far more interesting, less as a history of Jack's drinking habits than as a confession of the white logic of his despair. Already unable to sleep because of the pain of his diseases and his remedies for them, he was forced toward self-analysis in the depths of the night. He had to examine the contradictions within himself, he had to look at the tenuous links between his nature and the heroic myth that he tried to live. His process of self-awareness had begun.

In the last month of his life, shocked by the death of his favorite Shire stallion, Jack finally recognized his condition in notes for a novel about the dead stallion and for a short story to be called "Forty Horses Abreast." The notes speak of a wasted scholar, racked with pain, who studies through the night and lives vicariously through his mighty stallion. Yet his mind is capable of driving forty horses abreast, of holding together forty contradictory creatures in a leap toward illumination. The mind is able to do everything, if only the strength of the frail body can hold itself together against the pain.

Yet the pain proved too great. In the early morning of November 22, 1916, a few weeks short of his forty-first birthday, he took an apparent overdose of morphine and atrophine, a derivative of belladonna. He had used similar drugs for years to relieve his pain and to help rid himself of the toxins building up in his kidneys and bladder. He had to relieve himself every few hours through the night, or else the toxins would remain inside him and damage him severely. But belladonna is a beautiful and treacherous lady. A little of it stimulates the muscles of the bladder, while a lot of it closes them.

Trying to cure himself of a sudden spasm of acute pain, Jack injected himself with too much of the drug mixture and stopped his bladder from working. Despite later assertions that he did not die of uremia and that the death certificate was false, it is probable that he did die of the toxins in his bladder. As for the question of whether the overdose was an act of suicide or not, the answer is that the act does not seem to have been intentional, given the plans Jack had for the immediate future. The question is academic, in any case. Jack London was practically a walking corpse throughout the last months of his life. All the witnesses spoke of his slow poisoning, of a fat body, of a gray complexion, of an unnatural irritability—the signs of arsenic in his system from salvarsan. Only his powerful will and his dreams for the future of his ranch had kept him going at all.

His reputation as a man and as a writer eroded after his death. He had to be alive to speak fully through his words. His image was as mighty as his pen, if not mightier. What he left behind him was the myth that a writer should live what he describes. Jack always complained that he had little imagination, so that he had to take his plots from his own experience or the newspapers. He could also have said that he strove to realize his dreams, not to analyze them. As he seemed to be larger than life, he wanted to do more than other men did. Action to him was more satisfying than fiction. "Personal achievement, with me," he wrote, "must be concrete. I'd rather win a water-fight in the swimming pool, or remain astride a horse that is trying to get out from under me, than write the great American novel."

He did not write the great American novel, although he did write some good ones and some great short stories. He did, however, create the myth of the great American novelist. Still, it was not an entirely self-conscious creation. He thought himself to be exactly what he appeared to be. If his torments and tensions were hidden by his myth of himself, it was no bad thing; for a man who has a heroic myth of himself can achieve more than a man who knows himself too well and is afraid to move. To deny weakness, to insist on excess and success, is to live at full stretch. Jack London lived nine lives and wrote more than fifty books and died young. A man like that is worth his own myth—and his contradictions.

Andrew Sinclair, a novelist and former screenwriter, is the author of The Emancipation of the American Woman, *as well as biographies of Dylan Thomas and Warren G. Harding.* Jack, *his biography of Jack London, will be published by Harper & Row in the autumn of this year.*

READERS' ALBUM

HIGH CAMP

Shriners on a picnic? No, just the Wyman Comedy Company—an itinerant Western theatrical troupe of the last century—posed in the summer of 1882 amid the splendors of California's Yosemite Valley. Bridalveil Falls provides the dramatic backdrop for this vintage photograph, sent to us by John P. Talbot of Lodi, California, grandnephew of Rose Graham, seated at the right. Faded press notices from her scrapbook chronicle the successes of the troupe in small towns from southern California to British Columbia. The actors were enthusiastically received everywhere they performed, but it was apparently the dogs that stole the show. Placid, even somnolent, off stage, Rover (left) and Mose (far right) evidently became raving fiends in the flicker of the gaslights, lunging after Eliza with awful realism as she fled across the ice in *Uncle Tom's Cabin.* A jittery correspondent for the Bodie *Miner* went backstage to see for himself just how fierce they really were. From a "highly elevated position out of the way of the dogs during their scene," he pronounced them "in earnest in every move they make on stage." Ned, the perky dog posed next to the prop cookfire, was even more accomplished. "To hear that canine warble 'Baby Mine,' " reported the Chico *Record*, "would cause some of our amateur vocalists to blush."

* * * * *

We continue to invite our readers to send us unusual, dramatic, or "what's going on here?" photographs—at least thirty years old—that they own. They should be sent to Geoffrey C. Ward, American Heritage Publishing Co., 10 Rockefeller Plaza, N.Y., N.Y. 10020.

As we cannot be responsible for original material, we request that a copy be sent at first. Under no circumstances should glass negatives be mailed. Pictures can be returned only if accompanied by a stamped, self-addressed envelope. AMERICAN HERITAGE will pay $50.00 for each one that is run.

CROSSWORDS IN HISTORY — The Old West

by Eugene T. Maleska

Solution in the next issue

ACROSS

1 Cattle-entangling weapon
5 Covered or Conestoga
10 Hay carts
15 The—Lands of the West
18 Love, to a ranchero
19 Rush, in the Southwest
20 One of the Fords
21 Garden of the Gods site: Abbr.
22 Zola heroine
23 National Park in Wyoming
25 Step—(hurry)
26 Doctrines
28 Presuppose
29 Town in NW Michigan
31 Food of the Digger Indians
33 Caballero
35 Cowboy's milieu
36 English cafés
39 Crusoe's creator
41 Stagecoach robber, e.g.
44 Managed, as a ranch
45 Part of a chair back
47 Victimized by a scorpion
49 Pepper pot soup ingredient
50 Therefore
52 Yosemite Falls, e.g.
54 Gets wind of
56 Vehicle at Aspen or Alta
57 Appears
59 Giggle
61 Mare, to a stallion
63 A summer baby
64 Talks like a cowboy
66 Toots' kin
68 River in E. Texas
70 Yesterday, in Paris
71 Metal tag on a shoelace
72 Cowgirl-singer, — Evans
73 Volcanic peak in Calif.
75 El —, famed artist
76 Fastening devices
79 G.I.'s overseas address
80 Executive dress
82 Beethoven's "Third"
84 Maxi-like robe
86 Buffalo fish
88 "Oro y —," Montana's motto
90 Uses an iconoscope
92 Dwarf: Comb. form
93 The Snake River — in 23-Across
95 Founder of the Mormon Church
97 — a fox
99 Call — day
100 First months, in Mexico
102 Go cycling
104 Native of the Treasure State
106 Wilder's "The Skin — Teeth"
108 Sleazy saloons: Slang
110 McKinley's birthplace
111 Sheriff's aides
114 Nevada mecca, for short
116 Talk it over
119 Kind of school: Abbr.
120 Custer's last foe
123 Noxious weed on range lands
124 Name on a green stamp
125 Wooden comedian
126 Cow in old ads
127 "Monarch of — survey"
128 Pacific herb
129 Cosmetician Lauder
130 Raw and New
131 Timetable, for short

DOWN

1 Judge's bench
2 Actor Sharif
3 Traveler with Tonto
4 Tilled lands in the Southwest
5 Resting places for the Pony Express
6 Gorilla
7 Chugalug
8 Bases of columns
9 Caught with a lasso
10 Zane Grey book: 1937
11 Bulldogging is one
12 Get — the ground floor
13 Forty-— (gold seeker)
14 Cowhand's smoke
15 Dam in Columbia River (NW Oregon)
16 What little G.W. couldn't tell
17 Be foolishly fond
21 Mountain lions
24 California products
27 Intensified exclamations
30 "He hath spread — for my feet"
32 Emulates young Lincoln
34 Gay deceiver
36 Three in Taxco
37 Auriculate; ansate
38 Undershrub of the West
40 Hindu gift
42 Musketeers' foils
43 Change the decor
46 In—(certain): Slang
48 Gorgeous gorge
51 President Ford's birthplace
53 Watershed in the Rockies
55 What rustlers do
58 Sutter's ancestors
60 Angler for congers
62 Fanfare
65 Abate
67 Non-complainers
69 Typical Western hero
73 Country that first got to the West
74 Film about cowboys
77 Prairie dwellers
78 Clara or Barbara
79 Ranch unit
81 Pack tobacco in a pipe
83 Unflappable
85 Cowboy's horse
87 Gift to a dance-hall girl
89 Restrained a dogie
91 Black snakeroots
94 Pollution factor
96 Sort of port
98 Historic town in Normandy
101 French for 58-Down
103 Word with bow or cross
105 Dido's beloved
107 Checks a cayuse
109 Pine marten
111 Antelope's playmate
112 Critic Faure
113 Word on a proof
115 "Book of Esther" setting
117 La fille
118 Texas Rangers' activity
121 Three, in Torino
122 "Diamond —"

GIT ALONG, LITTLE GOATIE, GIT ALONG

It will be recalled that our "Readers' Album" in June of this year featured a photograph of an outsized rooster hitched up to a small wagon. Now we offer a period photograph of a billygoat hitched to a miniature sulky. The picture was taken in 1907 on the long-gone Casino grounds at Newport News, Virginia, and was sent to us by James A. Leftwich of La Jolla, California. The happy five-year-old decked out in his Buster Brown suit is Mr. Leftwich himself.

This whole business may start a trend in unearthing similar photos of unusual hitches that delighted youngsters long ago. Who knows the bounds of parents' imaginations? We can scarcely wait for a picture of a tiny buckboard being towed by a team of snails.

WILL THE MYSTERY GUEST SIGN IN, PLEASE

We invite our readers to guess how the father of our country signed his name. Was "George Washington" or "G. Washington" the form he customarily used? If you thought it was the first version, you were dead wrong. So were we.

In February, 1977, we ran a story about Nellie Custis, G. Washington's step-granddaughter. With it, we included a letter of advice from Washington embellished with a copy of what we assumed was his signature.

Not so, as Donald Jackson, former editor of the Washington papers and author of the article, pointed out to us:

"It's a fine issue.... But note that the facsimile signature on page 84 of my story is *not* that of George Washington. It is a crude imitation, probably done by some clerk in making a contemporary copy of a Washington letter."

George Washington

THE TVA: CHEAP, CHEAPER, CHEAPEST

James Branscome's "The TVA: It Ain't What It Used to Be," which appeared in our February, 1977, issue, brought us the following communication from John Kane of Rancho Palos Verdes, California:

"Twice comments were made to the effect that TVA sells power at a much lower cost than commercial utilities. The impression made was that this was because of superior management or lesser greed. Neither explanation is true. TVA can sell power for less because it does not have any of the financial expenses that any competing utility would have. Here is a partial list:

"Taxes. Taxes amount to as much as twenty per cent of the revenues of some utilities.

"Dividends. Public companies must pay a return to the people who put up the money. Unless, of course, they are a government agency.

"Interest costs. TVA bonds, as obligations backed by the American taxpayer, are rated AAA. This means that on a typical $100,000,000, 30-year bond, TVA will pay about $60,000,000 less interest than a public utility.

"The money value of other federal subsidies, direct and indirect, would be difficult or impossible to measure. The wonder is not that the TVA's cost of power is so low; the wonder is that it is so high."

On this long-familiar question concerning public vs. private power, Mr. Branscome replies:

"Mr. Kane's letter makes several points about TVA's finances and power that have long been favorites of agency critics. The facts are, however, that TVA in many instances is at a disadvantage relative to private utilities when it comes to tax breaks. For example, TVA gets no tax credits for installing pollution control equipment, as private utilities do.

"Tax breaks for private utilities have become so lucrative that the last study of the TVA system in 1974 by the CPA firm of Coopers and Lybrand concluded that had the agency been a private utility it would have paid no federal income taxes in the previous ten years. As the study notes, private utility income taxes have been declining over the last decade. TVA does, however, pay back to the government each year what amounts to a 'tax' based on the government's previous investment. It also pays in lieu of taxes (five per cent of revenue) to counties impacted by its facilities.

"So far as bond ratings are concerned, New York City's financial disaster should teach us that government entities have no sacred bond rating just because they are government related.

"TVA sells power more cheaply, as the article made clear, because it is close to the coalfields, buys coal more cheaply, and has more dams than most utilities with which to generate power. Additionally, no TVA official gets those $100,000-plus salaries so common in the utility industry.

"Seventy-five per cent of TVA's costs are for fuel. If the agency deserves criticism, it is for buying that too cheaply, and not for some imagined tax breaks."

Building a Dam, FROM A THREE-PART MURAL BY WPA ARTIST WILLIAM GROPPER. DEPARTMENT OF THE INTERIOR MURAL

FIND A TREE AND CUT IT

Sooner or later, the last report of a bicentennial aberration will reach us. Until then, we continue to feel it a moral obligation to keep our readers in touch with some of the stranger things that went on out there during the country's two hundredth birthday.

Take, for example, the triumph over one of nature's wonders that occurred in Pioneer, Ohio, a town of some one thousand souls. Pioneer, it seems, has been noted over the years for the unusually fine black walnut trees in its vicinity—especially *one* tree. It was estimated to be somewhere between 180 and two hundred years old and, inevitably, was dubbed the "Bicentennial Tree." Described as the most perfect black walnut tree in the nation, it stood more than 130 feet high, and its first 57 feet rose as straight and true as a Grecian column. "It was majestic," Ohio state forest officer Roger Herrett rhapsodized to a *New York Times* reporter. "I've seen perfect logs 20 feet long, but to have this perfectness spread over 57 feet, well, as old George Gobel said, 'They don't make them kind anymore.' "

The "Bicentennial Tree" was regarded with such enthusiasm that in December, 1976, its owners put it up for sale. The lucky purchaser, the Atlantic Veneer Corporation of Beaufort, North Carolina, placed its value at $30,000, a company spokesman exclaiming, "I've known about this tree for fifteen years . . . it is very unlikely that there would be another one like this, very unlikely." The tree was forthwith cut down, its perfect trunk bedecked with a suitably patriotic ribbon, and then shipped off to the company's plant, where it was scheduled to be sliced into two thousand board feet of walnut veneer, almost enough, the *Times* remarked, to cover three acres of land. Precisely *which* three acres was not noted.

NEW YORK TIMES PICTURES

ISRAEL'S DEBT TO ANDREW JACKSON

EDDIE JACOBSON AND FRIEND. *Kansas City Star*/HARRY S TRUMAN LIBRARY, INDEPENDENCE, MO.

During the behind-the-scenes infighting and debate that preceded President Harry Truman's decision to recognize the new state of Israel in 1948, as recounted by Clark M. Clifford in our April, 1977, issue, so much pressure was put on Truman that for a time he refused to see any Zionists, including the ailing Dr. Chaim Weizmann, who was soon to become Israel's first president and had journeyed to America to plead with Truman for recognition. But on March 12, Eddie Jacobson, Truman's old friend and former business partner in Kansas City, Missouri, called on the President in the White House to intercede for Weizmann. Four years later, Jacobson described the meeting in a letter he wrote to Dr. Josef Cohn of the Industrial Institute of Israel. A copy of that heretofore unpublished letter was recently sent to us by Loeb H. Granof, whose father, A. J. Granof, was a friend of both Cohn and Jacobson, as well as of Truman.

In his account, Jacobson noted that during the first part of the meeting Truman was extremely bitter over the attacks made on him by American Zionist leaders, and he steadfastly refused to see Weizmann. "I suddenly found myself thinking," Jacobson wrote, "that my dear friend, the President of the United States, was at that moment as close to being an anti-semite as a man could possibly be. . . ." And then: "I happened to rest my eyes on a beautiful model of a statue of Andrew Jackson . . . which I had noted passingly many previous times I had been to the White House. I then found myself saying this to the President: 'Harry, all your life you have had a hero. You are probably the best read man in America on the life of Andrew Jackson. . . . Well, Harry, I too have a hero. . . . I am talking about Chaim Weizmann. He is a very sick man, almost broken in health, but he traveled thousands and thousands of miles just to see you and plead the cause of my People. Now you refuse to see him because you were insulted by some of our American Jewish leaders. . . . It doesn't sound like you, Harry, because I thought that you could take this stuff they have been handing out to you. . . .'

"Just as I finished, I noticed that the President began drumming on his desk with his fingers and as I stopped talking, he abruptly turned around while still sitting in his swivel chair and started looking out the window. . . . I knew the sign. I knew that he was changing his mind. I don't know how many seconds passed in silence, but it seemed like centuries. All of a sudden he swiveled himself around again, facing his desk, looked me straight in the eyes and then said the most endearing words I had ever heard from his lips: 'You win, you baldheaded son-of-a-bitch. I will see him.' "

THEY WEREN'T NO DUMB CLUCKS

Why on earth would a band of seafaring Vikings have traveled all the way to Minnesota in the heart of North America in 1362? The notion that they did may seem absurd, but ever since the turn of the century many people have argued learnedly that it happened. They have based their claim largely on the Kensington Rune Stone, a flat rock incised with medieval Norse symbols that was allegedly discovered in 1898 on the Kensington, Minnesota, farm of a Swedish-American settler named Olaf Ohman.

Despite inconclusive studies and tests of the stone and its inscription, most serious scholars long ago decided that it was almost certainly a hoax, and they identified the likely culprits as Ohman himself, who had a resentment against better-educated people, and Sven Fogelblad, a hard-drinking local schoolteacher and cynic. Now, a series of tape recordings made in 1967 and recently released by the Minnesota State Historical Society not only corroborate that belief, but expose a third participant in the hoax—John P. Gran, one of Ohman's Scandinavian-born neighbors, who apparently also loved a good joke as much as he, too, despised educated folk.

OLAF OHMAN AND THE KENSINGTON RUNE STONE.
MINNESOTA HISTORICAL SOCIETY, ST. PAUL

The following selections from the tapes, published in the winter, 1976, issue of *Minnesota History*, illuminate the shenanigans of the trio. Describing the hoax were Walter Gran and Anna Josephine, the son and daughter of John P. Gran; the interviewer was Walter's nephew:

NEPHEW: Did you ever know him [Fogelblad]?

WALTER: No, I didn't get to know him, but Fogelblad, you see, was an outcasted minister from Sweden.... A regular drunkard.... But he was educated... well, he spoke seven languages, so you see he wasn't no dumb cluck.... And then you know when hard times come... that's when he used to come up here and stay with Ohman... he was the head man to lay out this inscription....

ANNA: Wasn't Papa and Ohman working together on the Larson place and while they were resting and having lunch, Mr. Ohman... carved out some script letters and he asked Papa if he knew what it meant?

WALTER: Oh yeah, he took out his jackknife and he was setting there and he carved some runic letters... and says now wouldn't it be fun... to make some scripts that would bewilder the whole community and the people, he said, and especially them that was educated. He was mad at people who were really educated.

ANNA: Why, he had no use for them.

WALTER:... Well, anyway, you know for a good hoax like that, Dad was in for them tricks....

NEPHEW: Well now, did Ohman ever admit that he did this?

WALTER: No, Ohman didn't. Well, you see, then as time went on, Papa was getting older and older.... He brought up about the rune stone.... He says, you know it is false, he says....

ANNA: You see, Papa was left-handed... and Ohman was right-handed.

WALTER: You know I seen that sculpture had been examined and it said it had been two men working on that stone and because one was a left-handed and one a right-handed man. Well, that fitted in for Dad and Ohman, but then I thought, by God it is something isn't it?

P	A	U	L		F	R	O	N	T		G	A	T	O	R		S	T	A	B
A	M	M	O		E	E	L	E	R		A	D	O	R	E		P	E	L	E
R	O	B	U	S	T	E	L	L	I		L	O	U	I	S	V	I	L	L	E
D	R	O	G	H	E	D	A		P	R	O		R	O	T	A	T	I	O	N
			R	O	D	E		S	L	O	O	P		N	U	M	B			
A	S	T	O	R		D	E	T	E	S	T	E	R		P	O	A	C	H	
G	E	E	Z	E	R		L	E	T	S		P	O	S		S	L	O	A	N
A	L	D	A		E	F	L	A	T		A	T	O	P			L	O	G	E
S	A	W		A	V	R	I	L		K	L	A	N	I	S	M		P	A	T
P	H	I	L	L	I	E	S		B	O	I	L	E	R	M	A	K	E	R	S
		L	I	L	L	E		P	E	R	A	K		A	U	G	E	R		
W	I	L	L	I	E	K	E	E	L	E	R		E	L	D	E	R	S	O	N
A	N	I		E	R	I	T	R	E	A		D	R	E	G	S		T	C	U
N	D	A	K			C	H	U	M		H	O	R	D	E		F	O	U	R
T	I	M	E	R		K	O	S		S	A	D	O		S	C	O	W	L	S
	A	S	N	E	R		S	E	N	A	T	O	R	S		A	R	N	I	E
			T	S	A	I		R	A	F	T	S		E	S	N	E			
S	C	O	U	T	I	N	G		V	E	R		C	A	N	I	S	I	U	S
C	I	N	C	I	N	N	A	T	I		I	D	A	H	O	S	T	A	T	E
A	N	A	K		E	E	R	I	E		C	O	V	E	R		E	M	A	R
D	E	N	Y		D	R	O	P	S		K	E	E	N	E		R	A	H	S

Solution to the June Crossword Puzzle

NOTE: Unfortunately, while crediting the photographs that accompanied our April, 1977, article on diners to their owner, Richard J. S. Gutman, we failed to make clear that our text was adapted from Mr. Gutman's research for a book he has written with Elliott Kaufman and David Slovic, to be published this fall by Harper & Row.